Writing and Understanding Poetry for Teachers and Students

Writing and Understanding Poetry for Teachers and Students

A Heart's Craft

Suzanne Keyworth and
Cassandra Robison

ROWMAN & LITTLEFIELD
Lanham • Boulder • New York • London

Published by Rowman & Littlefield
A wholly owned subsidiary of The Rowman & Littlefield Publishing Group, Inc.
4501 Forbes Boulevard, Suite 200, Lanham, Maryland 20706
www.rowman.com

Unit A, Whitacre Mews, 26-34 Stannary Street, London SE11 4AB

British Library Cataloguing in Publication Information Available

Library of Congress Cataloging-in-Publication Data
Keyworth, Suzanne, 1948–
  Writing and understanding poetry for teachers and students : a heart's craft /
Suzanne Keyworth and Cassandra Robison.
    pages cm
  Includes bibliographical references.
  ISBN 978-1-4758-1406-4 (cloth : alk. paper) — ISBN 978-1-4758-1407-1
(pbk. : alk. paper) — ISBN 978-1-4758-1408-8 (electronic) 1. Poetry—
Authorship. 2. Poetics. I. Robison, Cassandra. II. Title.
  PN1059.A9K49 2015
  808.1—dc23

                                                         2014044527

Printed in the United States of America

Contents

Preface   vii

Acknowledgments   xi

1   Some Initial Thoughts on Poets and Poetry,
    Workshopping Poems, and the Creative Process   1

2   Beyond the Ordinary: Witnessing the World as a Poet   13

3   Imagery: Getting to the Heart of It   23

4   Metaphors and Symbols: Finding and Using
    Creative Analogies   33

5   Line Endings, Turns, and Epiphanies: More Essential
    Elements of Craft   45

6   The Speaker and the Reader: A Dialogue   57

7   Narrative Poetry: Poems That Tell Stories   69

8   Communicating Emotional Truths and Avoiding Melodrama   85

9   Writing in Other Voices   97

10 Sound Devices   111

11 Punctuation: A Surprisingly Creative Tool   123

12 Effective Titles: Hints at Theme   133

13 Nature as Muse   143

14 The Prose Poem: A Revelatory Form 153

15 Writing in Various Forms 163

16 Portfolios, Presentations, Aural Modeling, and Syllabi 173

Brief Literary Biographies of the Poets 181

Preface

"Go now and do the heart-work," wrote Rainer Maria Rilke in *Letters to a Young Poet*. That's where the title of our book comes from, and its essence is about learning to do the heart work of writing poetry. Throughout the book, powerful poems serve as models of *how poems create meaning* and what devices they use in the craft. What sets it apart from other textbooks on learning to write poetry is its inherent philosophy of learning merged with the artistry of model poems.

This book is the creative combination of two poets' and professors' minds and hearts drawn from nearly half a century of combined experience. It offers a unique and student-friendly method of learning how to become a poet.

Writing and Understanding Poetry for Teachers and Students: A Heart's Craft allows readers and students to sample great writing, to understand meaning, and to understand how meaning is made by poets. Meaning is made through poetic sensibility and using the tools of the craft.

We want students to understand poetry by reading well; from that knowledge, they learn to write strong, well-crafted poems of their own. Our methodology evolves from a respect of the craft of poetry. How a poem works, how it uses elements of craft to create meaning, are as important as what a poem means, particularly to the poet. Writing poetry without the mastery of craft would be like picking up a cello and making noise without knowing anything about music, notes, tone, meter, or the singular beauty of its stirring strings.

Thus our book focuses on modeling some great poems, the analysis of those poems, and the aspect of "craft"—what a poem means, how it comes to meaning, how it delivers meaning, how it moves and develops meaning. Step by step, chapter by chapter, this text guides students of poetry to a deep and broad understanding of the elements of poetic craft. In the book, students learn the art of writing poems by reading explications of great poems that illustrate various fundamental elements of poetic craft.

Our premise is this: The art of poetry is grounded in craft and elevated by sensibility. Like the scaffold for a roof, craft is the underpinning of the poem. Craft is comprised of many "tools" the writer can use that include figurative and rhetorical devices plus elements of prosody and sensibility. Whether it is an image, a metaphor, a line break, a title, or an abstract sentence, all of these possible craft elements enable the poet to build the poem from the bottom up.

Our second premise is this: The art of poetry can and should be taught using the same kind of sound pedagogy that underlies all effective learning. Our chapters move from unit focus (and terms) to modeling and guided application (and experimentation). We offer critical reflections to round out meaning; we write explications for each model poem for discussion and expository example. Each chapter is scaffolded to build learning, explicitly and implicitly.

This book offers some useful advice on the creative process, including finding and generating ideas, revising, and producing final drafts to share and publish. It offers advice and examples in every chapter.

Our philosophy of teaching is founded on the concept of creating an atmosphere where everyone feels safe, an environment we call "our hearts in a safe place." Learning to workshop means learning to treat others with respect, to use the language of the creative process and its tools, and to participate in a particularly active fashion that helps learning, one's own and others' as well.

Our book is different from others on the market in another critically important way. Every chapter ends with a sampling of student poems written during workshops that used these chapters and their exercises and assignments as prompts. You will note the student poems sometimes follow the directions of a given assignment and sometimes wander off, but they illustrate emerging poets and people of growing sensibility to poetic art. Some of these poems went on to be published and also win state awards for college student poets.

We think our perspective is both interesting and useful, that readers will come away with a stronger sense of what poetry is, how it works, and how to craft it well. This book is written as a guide for teachers of poetry at all levels.

This textbook is written for those who want to understand poetry and those who teach it in a variety of environments, not just classrooms. Students of literature classes can use this book to learn how to explicate poetry. Emerging poets can utilize the book to build a foundation of craft. Lovers of poetry can simply read it, learn more about poetry, and enjoy poetry even more.

Acknowledgments

We thank all our wonderful students throughout the years for their contributing work in this volume and for all we learned from them. They made our "work" a joy and kept our teaching fresh and heartfelt. We thank our own teachers through the years, those who taught us well both deliberately and incidentally.

We thank especially two remarkable students who served as editorial assistants for this book, Allison Weatherly and Peggy Aiello. Both are gifted and unique people; several of their poems are included in the student samples as well. Both did some quality work as assistant editors on this textbook. Really, without you both and all the students over the years, this book could not have been written.

Chapter One

Some Initial Thoughts on Poets and Poetry, Workshopping Poems, and the Creative Process

A poem begins with a lump in the throat, a home-sickness or a love-sickness. It is a reaching-out toward expression; an effort to find fulfillment. A complete poem is one where the emotion has found its thought and the thought has found the words.

—Robert Frost

As art students know, one of the most effective techniques for learning any art form is to study the masters first. How do the greatest poets put together a poem? What techniques of sound and sense do they use? How are their poems constructed? How do their finest poems make meaning? If no rules exist exactly, poets can learn techniques—tools of the craft—to write strong poems.

This book is based on the premise that the craft of poetry can be learned by modeling. Poet Mary Oliver says, "I think if imitation were encouraged much would be learned well. . . . Before we can be poets, we must practice; imitation is a very good way of investigating the real thing" (Oliver, 13).

Craft is the scaffolding that supports the poem. Without craft, a poem fails. Every chapter in this book is geared toward learning the craft of poetry by studying the masters' works through the explication of poems, one by one. Each explication is supported by terms to study and know and followed by a modeling exercise.

LEARNING FROM MASTER
POETS OR MASTERFUL POEMS

When we say "masters" we mean "fine" writers, writers who have mastered the craft of writing and the curious and amazing art of poetry. Among those selected as "fine poets" are some most students of poetry will know and some they will not. Of course, many students think of Homer, Shakespeare, Wordsworth, Tennyson, Eliot, for example, when they think of master poets. But there are twentieth- and twenty-first-century master poets too. We have included many.

WHAT IS A STRONG POEM?

When readers respond to a poem, they frequently say "I like that!" (or conversely, I don't). But what do we all mean by liking a poem? Why do we like some poems? What makes a poem that resonates with readers? We call effective, resonant poems, strong poems.

A *strong poem* is one that meets certain criteria of excellence in sound, design, and ultimately meaning. It is not an enigma only the writer can grasp or an emotional plumbing of self. It is rather a work that shows unique sensibility in observing the world, that places a segment of that observation on the page in image after well-chosen image, that trusts the unconscious and the subconscious ability to create abstract connections and allusions, and that in showing mastery of the various poetic "tools," offers readers a fresh and sometimes startling new witness to being in the world.

Poetry is essentially philosophy and art, yet at the same time it seeks not to moralize but to share experience. The reader is left with that job of drawing the conclusions about what is right and what is wrong, what is shown about truth and what truths the poet expresses in the work.

A strong poem uses imagery to merge with emotion; the imagery employs the arts of metaphor, synesthesia, synecdoche, allusion, and other useful and essential tools. In addition, the strong poem has a heightened awareness of sound and ability to use sound devices of many kinds; it has a voice or speaker that draws readers in and pulls them along. In the end, the poem, image by image, re-creates a world of experience and shows it to us so that we are forever changed.

PORTFOLIOS: PRESERVING AND SHARING WORK

This book recommends the creation of portfolios, either hard copy or digital, of all work completed from all exercises during the semester. Many good reasons support this kind of preserving of one's work.

A portfolio can be a one-dollar Duo-Tang folder, a three-ring binder, a photo album filled with typed poems and photos, or a digital work shared electronically and/or printed in hard copy. The value exists in preserving, reflecting on, and sharing one's work. It's creative, and it's fun.

Most of all, it is a worthwhile endeavor to value one's artistry. It is a showcase for one's writing.

Portfolios can be used by instructors for evaluative purposes as well. Teachers can offer guidelines, rules, or be open to interpretation. It's entirely up to the teacher and the arrangement with his or her students.

Here are some good reasons to build a portfolio. One, poets can see themselves grow as writers from the struggle and lack of confidence in the initial exercises to the growing understanding of and use of craft in subsequent chapters, exercises, and poems. Second, students profit by revising poems copy by copy; sometimes, one poem may go through many drafts before it is "finished," whereas other poems will take just a little polishing. The *process* of writing is so important to becoming and being a poet. Finally, the portfolio displays and shares a poet's body of work. It takes the work seriously. It shows intent and learning. In many cases, portfolios can take the place of regular tests, quizzes, and any traditional type of "grading." It is all up to the instructor or facilitator.

THE CONCEPT OF MODELING

Just as the music student listens to the great musicians and tries to emulate them or learns the notes and time signatures that are the foundation of music, the student of poetry can learn from strong poems and masterful poets what poetry is, how it works, and what it can and should do.

This book, chapter after chapter, uses poets and poems as examples of primary poetic devices—the tools of the craft—and how to use them to write strong poetry. We learn from the masters, so to speak, by studying their work in the beginning. Ultimately, freed of the shyness of new artists and emboldened with trust in our tools and in our work, we create our own fresh work.

WELCOMING THE MUSE

One of the critical tools of craft any poet needs to master is how to welcome and hear the muse. Life is noisy; it is filled with the tyranny of the present, as some wise person once said. A writer (an artist, a musician, a sculptor, et al.) must carve out a time and place for writing and hearing the muse.

The muse might be defined as the creative voice alive and well inside you, a voice that has plenty to say when it begins to speak. Sometimes that muse hollers at us from the middle of the night or after a dream or when we are moved by something we see or feel. However, it can holler all it wants, but it will not create poetry (or any art form) unless it is heeded and unless it is given the time and silence to speak to us.

For all exercises in this book, we recommend writers create a personal spot away from the noise and demands of the daily world. It might be on a screened porch, in an attic room, or in an office with a door that locks. Metaphorically or actually, that door to the other world of real life needs to be locked while you call on the muse. This is hard advice to take, but it is absolutely necessary. Some writers may object that in their daily life it simply is not possible. It is possible and necessary.

Student writers of poetry should be encouraged to think of time in their muse space like good time spent working, shopping, cooking, or going to the gym. We all carve out time for such duties yet often fail to carve out a time and place for our own unique artistry.

We encourage our students to find a place that is safe and engenders peace in their spirit. They should make sure they are alone in this space and that no one will bother them. We encourage them to dare put up a sign on the "door" real or imaginary, "Do Not Disturb." Such thirty-minute muse space intervals can be rewarding and evoke images, thoughts, and poems that may never have been captured without them.

Some days, it's true, the muse may not speak at all; some days one's muse will speak so fast, a writer will have a hard time getting all the language down on paper. Think of this: There are poems waiting in our hearts and minds to be put down on the page. We must give ourselves quality time to honor them in this way. The creative self must be honored.

A JOURNALING IDEA

We recommend that creative writers begin to keep a faithful journal, a chronicling of ideas, images, and sensory experiences. Inexpensive or expensive journals are for sale in any good bookstore and also in Office Depot and such stores that sell supplies. Maybe writers will prefer a lined notebook or one without lines.

Many sizes and shapes are available. It's important to have a hard cover, as writers want something to write on when a desk isn't handy. Good pens are a must. Buy a few really nice pens, the kinds you like to hold in your hand, that welcome you to the act of writing in longhand. A pen can be one of the most important tools.

Some student writers swear they create on the computer alone (or one of the latest iPads or even a good smartphone), and that's fine, but things, good things, may get lost without a journal. Now, a journal is not a diary, not just a record of personal feelings. No. It is a professional venue meant to capture perspectives, unusual thoughts, and specific images.

These jottings may be used to create poems at a later date. Perhaps a great image or metaphor thought of on a drive home will be fleshed out into a poem later that night, or a dream recorded at midnight will become a poem in the morning. The important thing is to get the thoughts/ideas/ images down. Pay attention to sensory things—smells, colors, sights, sounds, textures—jot them down.

WORKSHOPPING ADVICE:
OUR HEARTS IN A SAFE PLACE

Workshopping means listening to critique from others with an open mind, learning not to get defensive (and that's hard sometimes!), and actually sifting through what others say to discover useful criticism to help you become a better writer.

And that isn't all, either.

Poets attend workshops to help them write better, to feel good about their work, to continue writing, and to offer support as a fellow writer.

Learning to critique and respond to the work of others is just as important as hearing feedback about one's own work.

Critique and *criticism* are powerful and positive words in workshopping. What group members notice, what the teacher says, and how everyone speaks are all critical components.

Workshops can be conducted in a number of ways, and teachers or facilitators will have their own ideas about this. Poems can be shared anonymously, authored, or a combination of both. Sometimes we like to workshop a number of poems anonymously during regular class times. In fact, this is a great way to get everyone's work critiqued while offering anonymity. We find writers like the feedback but are often shy at first; this kind of anonymous feedback can be really useful, especially early in group work.

Then, every few weeks, we might offer a "read-in," where poets choose one or two of their favorite poems and read them aloud to the class. Students can do this from a podium or in a circle of desks or chairs. We like the podium as poets learn to read their work, speak well in front of people, and in general add a bit of professionalism to their poetic lives. The group might invite others on such a night and offer refreshments. This kind of reading adds interest to any semester.

What does it mean to workshop a poem? It means to listen to the works of others with a critical mind, reflect on the work in a useful way, and offer feedback that will be helpful to the poem and to the poet. It is not just relevant to praise poem and poet with each work. It is the job of all serious poets involved in workshopping to be usefully critical, dutiful, and kind—dutiful to the art of poetry and kind to the poets themselves.

For anonymous workshopping, poems can be e-mailed or dropped off to the teacher/group facilitator by a deadline weekly. The poems will be transferred to a master copy and shown on a large screen in the classroom. Or each writer can type up and print enough copies for the entire class. The important thing is that feedback be impersonal, accurate, and helpful.

SOME HELPFUL IDEAS
ABOUT WORKSHOPPING POEMS

Try opening comments by stating something specific about the poem or noting the line structure, imagery, or word choices that are effective. Then note any questions or suggestions, offering it in language such as "In line 3, I am confused about this image . . . " or "maybe you could use only one adjective in line 7 rather than two." Keep it short, clear, specific, and craft-related. Think of how you yourself would prefer to hear and accept critique about your work; use that as a guideline as to how to communicate to others about their work.

WORKSHOP GUIDELINES TO SHARE WITH PARTICIPANTS

Create and sustain a nurturing environment. We call this "our hearts in a safe place." Everyone who learns to write and dares share work with others, usually strangers, needs to feel safe.

Create a pact with them on the first day so that all of your hearts are in a safe place. That is a ground rule established in week one: Nothing shared in the room of a personal, emotional nature needs to leave the room. No matter what is shared, other participants should show respect *and* be circumspect.

Address one thing you like about a poem before you offer critique or question. Be specific. Explain why and offer an example. When you speak in workshop, begin with the positive and follow with one specific suggestion for revision if you have one. It is your job to be productive and honest. It is your job to be a supportive critic.

Word your responses with sensibility; say something in a way you would like it said to you.

Keep the directions for each assignment in mind. Focus on them when you workshop any poem. Be specific and offer at least one example. Note the stanza and line number.

Don't offer empty praise. Be honest but kind to other writers sharing their work with you. While it is a scary thing to share one's work, it is also a thrilling experience sometimes. Remember that.

Remember it is a two-way street: you are there to offer critique and support the artist; you are there to hear critique and receive support as a writer. Don't turn off when the work of others is being workshopped.

Strive to become a good critic by finding what is good, unique, special, about a given poem and celebrating that; at the same time, zero in on weaknesses such as telling too much, being too vague and abstract, or using too many words.

Ask the right questions of each work. What is the work trying to do? What is it trying to capture? Note that in words. Does it achieve that end? If not, where might it improve? Is there something that strikes you as odd or out of place? Note that and explain why.

Use the poetic terms and rhetorical devices as you learn them. Use the terms to express yourself when speaking about poetry. The more you use the language of poetry, the more the tools become familiar and your own to use well.

Don't take it personally. It's about the work. Not everything you write is wonderful. Workshopping ideally is not just ego stroking. It is hard work to make poetry better, stronger, more literary and polished.

Try putting yourself in other poets' shoes.

Sometimes silence is the best reaction. If the group is quiet after your poem is first shared, don't be intimidated. Sometimes silence means the poem packed a real punch; your peers need time to gather their thoughts.

Remember writing is a process. Cull, edit, revise, add, replace, reread a dozen's dozen times. Some great poets say a poem is never finished.

Poetry is a beautiful thing, but it isn't a venue to bleed your feelings. Poetry is as much about control of emotion as it is about expression of feeling. Keep the melodrama. Use more restraint. Write from diverse points of views. Write about others. Be a witness of the world.

EXERCISES FOR STUDENTS

Quick Exercise 1. Freewriting Poetry to Call the Muse (15 minutes)

In your chosen spot, sit with pen and paper for ten minutes, looking out a window, around the room or place, or looking inward into your mind.

What do you see there? Poetry begins with concrete images—real things; things that can be seen, smelled, heard, touched, tasted, described in size, color, and shape. Jot down everything you see, creating a word picture on the page.

Do not editorialize. That means instead of writing down "a beautiful day" you write down "oblong clouds," "herringbone sky pattern," "purple crepe myrtle in bloom." Be specific and concrete. This kind of freewriting opens the door to creative expression. When you are finished, look back over your images. Think about what makes one "better" or more effective than another. Share a few with your group. Discuss reasons for your selection(s).

Quick Exercise 2. Developing Creative Analogies: A Harvest of Similes/Metaphors! (Instructor may bring a bag or basket of various fruits and vegetables to class.) (25 minutes)

Come up with some of your own. From the various fruits and vegetables, pick one or more. Hold it in your hand and your mind's eye. Examine it from all angles. Ask yourself, what does it look like? Feel like? Smell like? What is it *like*? Then write that down as a simile using the words *like* or *as* or a metaphor (omit *like* or *as*). GRAPE: "A darkly seamless voice overhead in a network of many." RAISIN: "Aged youth." Share your analogies with the class. Write them on the board perhaps. Discuss the thought process used in creating creative analogies like these. Remember this for future poems.

Quick Exercise 3. Workshopping a Poem (30 minutes)

Use the workshopping guidelines from a previous page in this chapter. Follow those guidelines to examine and analyze one or more of the poems at the end of this chapter and as a group, edit and revise the poem. Discuss the whys and wherefores of your decisions. Make sure you offer reasons for your decisions, as this sharpens your critical skills and your own knowledge of poetry craft. Focus on details.

THE MODEL EXERCISE

Pick a spot. Study one particular thing, a concrete thing like a stairway, a window, the field outside your window, yourself in the mirror. Maybe it is something you observed on your drive to or from this very class, a sight you might have passed by many times in the past and just not noticed. But today, you are a poet, and poets are noticers.

Stare at something long enough to create images and that come up with some greater understanding of the object or your own feelings. It can be serious or funny, or it can be a combination of both. Lay your images down on the page line by line in poetic format. Don't worry too much about line endings and do not use rhyme.

We have no "master poets" to model from in week one. Instead, read and study the student poems, Allison Weatherly's poem "If You Stare at Something . . . " and Peggy Aiello's "Dogwoods." Use these poems as your models. Try the one-stanza or the several-stanza poem written in tercets (three lines to each stanza). Don't worry about line count or rhyme.

When you have finished, leave the poem alone for a couple days. Come back and spend time editing and revising it. Polish it. Delete all extra words. Read it aloud to yourself and to others. Type it up and share it with your group at the next class meeting.

SAMPLE STUDENT POEMS

If You Stare at Something

by Allison Weatherly

Behind my tired blue stare
Lives an empty room.
It reads like coffee stained words,
From my favorite book, breathes
Like winter's bitter bite on my nose,
And listens like a bird's first song.
If only I could find the door.

Dogwoods

by Peggy Aiello

She drives along the familiar stretch of road
as the tangled branches begin to reveal
their truth. March has arrived as a lamb

or did she sleep through the lion's roar?
Perched precariously like snow
wisps on tips of branches—

as though a light breath of wind
might clear the bough of its illusion.
She passes and is reminded

of how deceivingly beautiful dogwoods
can be as they peep their perfect snowy
flowers out from naked branches.

REFERENCE

Oliver, Mary. *A Poetry Handbook: A Prose Guide to Understanding and Writing Poetry.* San Diego, CA: Harcourt Inc., 1994.

Chapter Two

Beyond the Ordinary

Witnessing the World as a Poet

> The work of the eyes is done. Go now and do the heart-work on the
> images imprisoned within you.

> —Rainer Maria Rilke, from *Letters to a Young Poet*

Because poetry stretches beyond the ordinary world of perception, we suggest it is "beyond the real" or "surreal" in nature. As defined by the artists, surrealism is a style of artistic expression that heeds and uses the subconscious or unconscious human mind, including dreams and dream-like imagery, as well as focuses on and creates imagery arrived at by unexpected juxtapositions. However, we do not apply the word *surrealism* as used in the past to describe art or any era of writing.

Instead, in this book, we use the word *surreal* simply, broadly, to describe the way poets examine and describe the world in an extraordinary fashion, one that makes unusual and fresh connections, leaps, and one that creates fresh understanding and insight.

Much of this is true of poetry in general; therefore, we frequently use the term *surreal* to describe the *beyond the ordinary* perception and creativity necessary in poetry. The reason we chose to begin the book this way is because it is a very strong element of poetic craft. It may indeed be part of the tradition of poetry throughout the ages as represented by various poets long before the twentieth and twenty-first centuries and long before it had a name. Consider Dante's descent into the circles of hell, for example, or Milton's dreamlike world in *Paradise Lost*.

Poetry implies the use of images that stretch beyond the ordinary into the extraordinary, beyond the rational image into the subtle tones of irrational thoughts bound up in an image. Poetry demands and includes imagery both concrete and literal as well as interpretive as it moves into the "other" realm of existence, into the place where the real meets the unreal and where the imagination takes a grand leap into the image of dreams or into our intuitive mind.

This is an important craft element that some of the great poets use in such a way as to make the poem carry the reader off into another imaginary world.

TERMS USED IN THIS CHAPTER

Allusion: An indirect reference to another work of art or literature, such as "On my own road to Damascus, I saw a light . . . ," an allusion to Saul's conversion to Christianity and his new life in Christ as Paul. An allusion can be an implicit mention or connection to another thing, person, or other known thing. The point is the allusion serves the theme of the poem in some relevant fashion.

Caesura: A poetic device in some ways opposite to enjambment. Caesura is the use of full-stop punctuation midline or in an unexpected place midpoem that forces readers to stop, pause, pay attention.

Enjambment: Enjambment is a device that encourages the reader to leap to the following line, usually through the use of no punctuation at line's end. As such, readers take no breath at line's end and understand the line "wraps around" to the next line for meaning. Both caesura and enjambment serve poets well in controlling pace and tone.

Craft: As used in this book, refers to the way a poet learns to employ the tools of poetry in order to create a poem of literary quality (in contrast to simplistic verse). As actors refer to their art as a "craft," poets master tools of craft to create art.

Image: The art of painting word pictures in a reader's mind, particularly useful in poetry. Images are created of concrete sensory experiences of sight, sound, smell, touch, taste, size, color, and shape.

Imagery: The poetic device created by the construction of images (see above).

Juxtaposition: The poetic (and rhetorical) device used to place two opposing ideas, thoughts, images, or feelings side by side in order to accentuate the difference between and the meaning of each.

Mood: The tone of any given part of a poem or entire poem (or work of literature). In most strong poems, the tone changes at least once, offering a contrast between two conflicting emotions or conditions.

Personification: The device of giving human qualities to a nonliving thing. Personification is different from anthropomorphizing in that the former is an obvious device to evoke an unusual comparison for poetic purposes while the latter is a philosophical or scientific fallacy.

Surrealism: A type of artistic expression that lends credence to dreamlike images and imagery of the unconscious/subconscious mind. Surrealism was an artistic movement begun in Europe in the early twentieth century. Its tenets or major points of belief are that the unconscious mind and the dreaming mind offer insights into being that can be expressed as art.

In this text, we do not mean to suggest that all poetry is surrealistic; we do suggest nonetheless that looking at the world as an artist demands a unique vision. *Surrealism* as we use the term allows the writer freedom to use all forms of emotional, physical, psychical, and dreamlike images and "truths." It allows art to be freed from the constraints of truth as provable and actual.

Theme: Theme is the totality of what a work of art means in its deepest and most complex sense. Theme is the result of the gestalt in any work of art, the sum of the equation, the intended as well as the serendipitous result, the connecting of all the dots. It is not what happens or whom it happens to but what all of those things mean.

THE MODEL POEM

Beginning

by James Wright

The moon drops one or two feathers into the field.
The dark wheat listens.
Be still.
Now.
There they are, the moon's young, trying
Their wings.

Between trees, a slender woman lifts up the lovely shadow
Of her face, and now she steps into the air, now she is gone.
Wholly, into the air.
I stand alone by an elder tree, I do not dare breathe
Or move.
I listen.
The wheat leans back toward its own darkness,
And I lean toward mine.

THE EXPLICATION

From his book *The Branch Will Not Break*, James Wright offers a poem titled "Beginning." If readers take a close look, they will discover the nature of the surreal image along with several other important elements of craft such as the one-word line, the layering of texture onto the page, important line breaks, personification, juxtaposition, a thematic title, and control of mood and pacing.

Wright begins this poem with this image: "The moon drops one or two feathers into the field." Imagine. There are feathers floating down from the moon in the air above the field. The speaker is standing there watching as if in amazement. Perhaps he did not know the moon embodied feathers, but in this curious world it does.

And in this moment the "dark wheat listens," and the entire world of human and natural existence turns its head toward the makings of the moon above, a surreal landscape where the human meets the weird freedom of imagination. Only in imagination can such an image begin and only in the soul can it be believed. This conveys the nature of the surreal image, a merging of the imagined with the real, the imaginary with the actual. Think about that for a moment.

The moment resonates with the speaker. He says, "Be still. / Now.", as if reminding himself to hush, pause, and listen just as he admonishes the reader to do the same. Wright brings the poem to a complete stop in the middle of the lines; this full stop midline is called "caesura," a powerful device of both sound and meaning.

The speaker *slows the pace* by first using a two-word command and then a one-word command so that the reader stops in midpoem and takes the whole first section into consideration. Surely this act performed by the moon must be serious, or why would the speaker stop the reader in midpoem?

The answer becomes obvious: because the speaker wants to make sure his reader recognizes the significance of this event. Not every day does the moon drop feathers into a field. Not every day does the world of spirit engage with the human world, the world of nature, which is also engaged in the moment.

We live in a mundane world, in a world of the ordinary, but Wright's world is anything but ordinary. He sees beyond the obvious into a broader view of the universe and what this universe has to offer us as human beings. He gives the reader a new vision and new hope for what tomorrow may bring. Notice the layering of texture and how Wright has taken the feathers and turned them into an image, a surreal image, of the moon's young. See how he stretches beyond the ordinary into the realm of the imagined.

Now Wright stretches the mind of the reader even further, far enough to include the image of something more. "Between trees, a slender woman lifts up the lovely shadow / Of her face. . . ." The poem has gone from the moon's young to the image of a "lovely" woman's face in the moonlight, a woman who "steps into the air. . . ." Perhaps the speaker is lonely, and in his loneliness he imagines this slender woman stepping out of the very ether around him into his world, but only for a brief moment.

Just for a moment she appears and then "she is gone. / Wholly, into the air." He lies stricken with just a glance of this imagined woman, the woman of his desire. And so the speaker stands in the dark field alone. Watching this event, he stands "alone by an elder tree," and does "not dare breathe / Or move" lest this vision disappear as it already has.

The poem has a total of fourteen lines, the length of a sonnet. But in this case some of the lines are only two words and one of the lines is only one word. We can't, therefore, call it a sonnet. In just a few short lines and even fewer words the poet manages to capture a newly imagined world.

Wright creates a title that reflects the poem's mood and meaning. The poem, titled "Beginning," obviously is the beginning of an adventure into the other world, the world beyond the ordinary realm into the extraordinary. In this world anything might be possible. Feathers drop from the moon, the moon has tiny young moons, and slender young women magically appear.

Wright ends this clever, daring poem with the lonely image of the wheat leaning "back toward its own darkness," and the speaker leaning back "toward mine," an image of longing. For a moment the world was alive and fleeting and the speaker was spellbound by the happenings in his life. His heart was lifted and his spirit was moved into longing for a woman who does not exist in our world, yet Wright creates her in such a way that the reader believes she does, in fact, exist.

So what happens in the end? The natural world and the human world revert back to the darkness of their place in the real world, that dark world of human existence. Beyond that existence, Wright suggests magic can be found, things we can only imagine, but things that are a special kind of "real" if readers open their eyes to them, otherworldly things, spiritual things.

EXERCISES FOR STUDENTS

Quick Exercise 1. Find the Magic in Personification and Imagery (15 minutes)

Spend fifteen minutes in class (or out!) working with the devices of personification and imagery. Examine (in your imagination or in the actual world) some *thing*. Create several personifications of what this thing might say, do, look like, things that of course are impossible in "reality" such as the sky frowning, a tree breathing, a room waiting for someone's return. List as many as you can. Think about them when you are done and choose a couple of your best ones to share with the class.

Quick Exercise 2. Leaping from the Concrete to the Abstract (15 minutes)

Brainstorm an idea of a poem with a title, but don't write the poem yet. Start with a title just for fun. Like Wright, imagine another kind of reality where magic occurs regularly. In your mind (or in actuality if you can leave the classroom), find a "spot" for this magical place. You can use a tree like Wright did to inspire him. Follow his lead. What drops from your tree? What imagery does your tree create? Imagine this spot as a place where any kind of magic can happen. Generate a list of details that are both concrete and abstract. Perhaps this will allow you to use personification.

THE MODEL EXERCISE

Write a short poem from five to ten lines describing a particular spot. Use the quick exercises to prompt you. Use Wright's poem as your model. Use the ideas you engendered in either one or both of the quick exercises or write an entirely new and different poem. Your goal is to create a poem that steps across the lines of real into the surreal and extraordinary, a poem that jumps back and forth between the possible and impossible, the actual and the imaginary.

See, read, think about, and perhaps discuss with others the sample student poems at chapter's end. Perhaps, for example, your poem will be a dialogue between you and some *thing* in nature's world, something impossible in the "actual" but not the extraordinary, surreal world of artistic perception.

You might use your imagination to place yourself at a moment from memory, a difficult or challenging moment, a moment that called up your courage and your kindness. Make sure you gather the same concrete details from memory as you would for a "real" spot.

It can be as simple as choosing a spot, writing down the details and descriptions. Then turn those details into imagery. Lay those images down line by line into some poetic form on the page. Do not try to rhyme any lines, please. Let this be a free-form poem in every respect.

Allow your poem to move beyond the ordinary in its fearless plumbing of the abstract world in the fashion of Wright's poem.

Here are some helpful guidelines: Find a point of observation. Begin your poem in a setting the reader will be able to see. Pretend you are an observer (or perhaps you really were) from a particular, concrete place like "I stand alone by an elder tree." Perhaps you encounter, either actually or imaginatively, an animal or a wild creature. *Begin with an image* like "The moon drops . . . " or "The sun showers down. . . ." It is generally good advice to begin with an image.

Consider the speaker. Who is telling your poem? Remember the speaker does not have to be you. Just think about who is speaking and to whom, with what kind of voice and tone?

Select well-chosen, strong verbs to show movement and add to the visual or sensory imagery you create. Free yourself and encourage yourself to look at the world as a surreal place where you may witness the ordinary and the extraordinary and where you may combine the two fearlessly.

When you put the images you have brainstormed on the page, consider your line lengths and line endings. Control the poem's pace by using pauses of two or more very short lines to create a kind of stop time.

To create imagery: Ask, what is happening here? Where am I transported in this moment? What does this scene make me think about? What connections can I make from past feelings or experiences? Be specific. Be concrete with sensory details: sight, sound, smell, touch, taste, size, color, shape, but don't overwhelm the poem with details. Choose the most unexpected details.

Complete your poem with a motion or an action or interplay between yourself and the images. End with a strong, concrete image. Do not tell the reader what to know or feel. Trust the image to speak for itself. Tread fearlessly into the surreal landscape, blurring the line between the real and the imagined. Title your poem something thematically suggestive, not obvious in the poem itself.

Let your poem lie for a day or two; return to it as a reader. Edit out any unnecessary words or phrases. Watch out for redundancy and eliminate it. Prune, prune, prune.

SAMPLE STUDENT POEMS

Magnolia Avenue

by Natalie Lyons

Miracle Mile jumped the tracks and spread to Union Station
where Greyhound bus riders and Amtrak train viewers wait
surrounded by manicured beauty of red brick buildings
accented with purple petunias and yellow alamanda vines.
DeeDee's Hot Dog House hung a new plastic sign
and a magenta awning to shade the sparkling window
that rattles when the train rumbles past.
The architect Andrew Copeland has spread

the good fortune across the street where the Avenue
divides. His stucco station with a barrel tile roof
fills the center of the "Y." Twin islands out front hint
at what used to be, round top gas pumps where attendants
with name tag patches sewn on their tucked-in shirts
ran to hear "fill-er-up" as customers sat
in the comfort of Fords and Chevys.
The miracle stopped at the Salvation Army building
where years ago ugly metal shutters rolled down
over plate glass windows—perhaps for a hurricane,
and no one since has taken them away. No flowers here,
only cigarette butts and those down on their luck litter
the parking lot. Next door Toffaletti's Hardware store,
where mom bought spatterware bowls and dad
bought nuts and bolts in odd sizes, has boarded the door
that held an Open/Closed sign hanging from a chain.

Intermission

by Shan Wimberly

The water oak reaches to grab heaven.
Peering through the branches
a lone wolf.
Waits.
The last brown leaf surrenders,
to the creeping leaves of three.
An old frail woman draped in red
points northward.
Her cape flows like the Red Sea
through the strait-narrowed way.
Thunder claps.
A branch from the water oak snaps,
ushering in my last curtain call.
The water oak, imperfect, extends
its reach to heaven.

NOTE

Credit: James Wright, "A Blessing" and "Beginning" from *Collected Poems* ©
1963 by James Wright. Reprinted by permission of Wesleyan University Press.

Chapter Three

Imagery

Getting to the Heart of It

Don't tell me the moon is shining; show me the glint of light on broken glass.

—Anton Chekhov

Poets use imagery like painters use color and paintbrushes. Imagery is the heart of poetry, and it is the essential tool of the craft. How does a poet choose an image? How does a certain image connect emotionally and meaningfully to the content of the poem? This connecting of emotion to the poem's content is deeply important to a poem's strength and beauty. An image is more than a picture created in the reader's mind. At its best, an image is a powerful tool for constructing and connecting with the emotional heart of the poem.

As stated in chapter 1's primary modeling exercise, the choice of imagery relies on concrete details (sight, sound, smell, touch, taste, size, color, shape) as well as leaps of mind into more abstract or beyond-the-ordinary metaphors. A strong poem conveys powerful imagery that sets the situation in time and place; it opens like a creative door into the poet's heart. The Imagists of mid-twentieth-century American poetry relied on imagery to convey experience, but poetry from any century uses imagery as its primary tool.

As poets examine their surroundings—both ordinary and beyond the ordinary—and begin to enter a poem, they must choose the details to convey in images. Remember to choose the unexpected details; surprise the reader with the beyond-the-ordinary perspective. Another good thing to remember is not to overwhelm the reader with too many images and too many details. Choose one or a few; make them powerful and unusual.

Finally, the imagery selected and conveyed in words will create its own tone, and this tone will influence meaning and what readers get from the poem. Throughout the process of editing and revision, it's important to remember that. But imagery contains more than this. American poet Mary Oliver says that poets have a responsibility to readers when choosing and delivering imagery because the images remain in the readers' minds thereafter.

When we coach emerging poets, we want to warn them to be careful about that; be daring and fearless, yes, we tell them; be accurate and detailed and go after the extraordinary details that create imagery, but remain aware *that art is a relationship with its public*. We need to encourage them to self-edit, although it can be painful as we come to love our own words and phrasings. Writers need to learn to weed and prune, weed and prune. The best poets achieve spare and pure imagery.

Most importantly, effective poems never tell readers how to feel, how they felt, how anyone should feel about the whole thing. The most effective poets—the master poets—don't explain. They trust the imagery; they expect readers to get it without any further explanation.

Such poets establish an intimate dialogue with their readers; they believe readers will see and hear and sense their imagery; they know the readers will take that leap at the end of the poem with them, from the literal to the figurative, from the concrete to the imaginative, without blinking.

TERMS USED IN THIS CHAPTER

Denotation/Connotation: Both terms have to do with definition and meaning of any word. While *denotation* means a dictionary and literal meaning, *connotation* implies the deeper figurative meaning associated with the use of a word.

Extended Metaphor or Poetic Conceit: In poetry, an extended metaphor that controls the entire poem from beginning to end is called a poetic conceit.

Irony: Irony is a sophisticated rhetorical device used in all of literature and composition/rhetoric. There are many types of irony, including but not limited to dramatic, situational, and cosmic ironies. Irony takes place when the opposite of what was expected or intended occurs, causing a sense of surprise and perhaps epiphany.

Stanza: A stanza is a poetic paragraph.

Terza Rima: From the Italian meaning "third rhyme," a fixed form of poetry using a series of tercets (three-line stanzas) with an interlaced end-rhyme pattern (ABA, BCB, CDC, DED, EFE, etc.).

Tone: Tone means the mood of a piece of text or a poem that conveys the speaker's emotion. It is primarily created by the choice of language, the syntax, and the speaker's attitude toward the poem's contents and toward the audience.

THE MODEL POEM

First Snow in Alsace

by Richard Wilbur

The snow came down last night like moths
Burned on the moon; it fell till dawn,
Covered the town with simple cloths.

Absolute snow lies rumpled on
What shellbursts scattered and deranged,
Entangled railings, crevassed lawns.

As if it did not know they'd changed,
Snow smoothly clasps the roofs of homes
Fear-gutted, trustless and estranged.

The ration stacks are milky domes;
Across the ammunition pile
The snow has climbed in sparkling combs.

You think: beyond the town a mile
Or two, this snowfall fills the eyes
Of soldiers dead a little while.

Persons and persons in disguise,
Walking the new air white and fine,
Trade glances quick with shared surprise.

At children's windows, heaped, benign,
As always, winter shines the most,
And frost makes marvelous designs.

The night guard coming from his post,
Ten first-snows back in thought, walks slow
And warms him with a boyish boast:

He was the first to see the snow.

THE EXPLICATION

Richard Wilbur's talent for creating images is illustrated in his poem "First Snow in Alsace." The images in this poem are full-bodied and extravagant, weaving deftly down through the poem.

The reader enters the poem through a startling image: "The snow came down last night like moths / Burned on the moon." The snow is compared to moths but not just any moths. These have been "burned on the moon"; thus the implication is burned moths, smoke, ashes, leftover and fading flame. So right away readers get a dark/light juxtaposition that suggests something terrible has happened recently but now the snow is falling. The snow is not quite clean, the reader senses; it is, rather, the color of burned moths. What is happening here? See how a well-drawn image leads a reader into a poem?

This burned snow "fell till dawn," but more importantly "Covered the town with simple cloths." Snow is a natural phenomenon, a part of nature in its glory; therefore, the snow is compared with "simple cloths," as if the making of snow by nature is a simple process, one that is able to cover the world like cloth covers the table. *Simple* can also be a noun that means an herbal remedy or a natural remedy. Thus the noun choice is a deft one.

In terms of craft, Wilbur rhymes the first line with the third line. It's a structured poem, a type called terza rima comprised of eight tercets and one single line. (Chapter 15 discusses more of these wonderful fixed-form poems.) It has an interwoven rhyme pattern of ABA as does the entire poem. To find the rhyme pattern, look at the final word in each line. Call the first rhyme A, the second B, and so forth. That's how you can chart the rhyme scheme.

The rhymes are graceful and unforced, so the poem moves smoothly down the page in three-line stanzas, except the last line, which stands on its own after a stanza break.

Wilbur continues with "absolute snow lies rumpled on / What shell-bursts scattered and deranged, / Entangled railings, crevassed lawns." The speaker begins to complicate the image of the snow by having it cover the remnants of brutal war and a recent battle in which "shell-bursts" lie "scattered and deranged"; railings are "entangled," lawns "crevassed."

Wilbur's use of the word *absolute* to describe this snow, and also *rumpled*, suggests that snow has the uncanny ability to cover over human carnage. The reader cannot help but think of a rumpled bed, a place of comfort. Wilbur's use of concrete images redefines our thoughts of what snow can do.

The reader also recognizes the juxtaposition of white and black, the opposites, which reflect both good and evil on a metaphorical level, or pristine white snow and the black marks left behind to scar the landscape on a literal level. In the next stanza the speaker personifies the snow, saying: "As if it did not know they'd changed, / snow smoothly clasps the roofs of homes / fear-gutted, trustless and estranged."

Here the snow fails to recognize the ravages of war on the houses in this town, and it covers the roofs as if everything is normal, but the houses remain "fear-gutted." Still, the snow attempts to cover all signs of war. The snow turns "ration stacks" into "milky domes," and the snow also manages to transform the "ammunition pile" into "sparkling combs."

Note how the poet juxtaposes destruction with salvation throughout this poem: The town is mangled, battered, and crushed by war, but those soldiers and no doubt civilians who survived the battle have awakened to a new world, it seems, a redeemed world.

Wilbur stacks the images of war one by one into the poem, then evokes the image of the snow filling "the eyes / Of soldiers dead a little while" just a mile or two away from the town. It is a curious line that suggests a field filled with dead soldiers lying on their backs and being covered with snow.

Wilbur does not comment on the war. He simply juxtaposes the white snow against the images of horror, which makes a comment all its own.

The poem tells us "persons and persons in disguise" are "walking the new air white and fine." Two interpretations are possible here: One is that some of the persons "walking" the air are ghosts now pure and redeemed; the other is that those who remain, now covered in snow as well as shocked by tragedy, appear shocked to be alive.

They are literally and figuratively changed by what has happened. It becomes both tragedy and miracle. They "trade glances quick with shared surprise." Wilbur's images accentuate the amazement of the people.

The snow creates a surreal and even miraculous vision of the world with its stark white snowdrifts. Even through "children's windows," "frost makes marvelous designs." The snow seems to redeem for a moment the people and children in this town, and even the soldiers passing through seem redeemed. The tone has changed from the weird, rust-colored snow and deranged landscape to one of peace, of hope, of beauty.

As the "night guard" comes "from his post," walking slowly, thinking about "ten first-snows back," he "boasts" "He was the first to see the snow." This simple moment shows an almost miraculous childlike innocence. One wonders who that night guard was; perhaps the poet himself? A night guard who spoke to the speaker? Is the speaker Wilbur himself? We don't know. And it doesn't matter. This poem has verisimilitude. The scene registers as true to readers. We believe this. We are transported by the poem's honesty and clarity of imagery.

Wilbur's use of powerful images here suggests that nature offers a kind of grace, a mystical healing of the ravages of war and the devastations caused by human beings at war. This grace is a kind of redemption. The poem's tone is so tender that it sounds almost hymnal in places.

Wilbur uses strong images created by an attentive eye, a writer on whom nothing is lost in his witnessing of it. He looks at the world or at the world of memory and from it withdraws one morning in which something miraculous seems to happen. Others notice this, but he, the poet, recorded it here, and more than that, he created images of sight, sound, smell, color, size, and shape.

EXERCISES FOR STUDENTS

Quick Exercise 1. Creating Imagery through Word Choice (15 minutes)

Look up the words *melancholy* and *despair* in a dictionary. It doesn't matter that you already know what the words mean; what matters is that the dictionary will often give you new insights into a common word. Ask a few questions: What is the difference between sadness and melancholy? Despair and melancholy?

Your task is to learn how to create imagery that expresses a particular mood. Brainstorm a list of images that capture the mood of the word *melancholy* and the word *despair*. Jot down your phrases. See if you can create images that suggest melancholy and despair without using those words. Share these phrases with the class or a writing partner at the end of fifteen minutes.

Quick Exercise 2. Brainstorm a List of Images about a Specific Place (15 minutes)

In your mind's eye, pick a place in nature or from your childhood. Make sure it is a specific and real place. Jot down details about that place. How did/does it smell there? What colors do you see? Concentrate on sight, sound, smell, touch, taste, size, color, and shape.

These are the kinds of details that create imagery. Remember what you learned in chapters 1 and 2 about a poet's perception. Think about Wright's imagery that moves back and forth between the real and the surreal; think about Wilbur's poem and how the imagery creates tone and mood from the first line. Remember not to offer the obvious but to notice and share the images others might miss.

Make your imagery startling, unique, and packed with meaning. List your images. If you have time, edit and polish them. Share with the class. Use this exercise to move into the modeling assignment below.

THE MODEL EXERCISE

Write a poem about nature's ability to heal the world in a particular place. It's important to choose one specific spot, not write about nature in general, which is too broad for details. Title your poem something that includes the name of the area, place, or region. Think about Wilbur's title and how it affects meaning.

Regarding the form and structure, you can try to write a rhymed poem, or try the challenging rhymed tercets (or unrhymed). Sometimes attempting end rhyme is awkward for emerging poets. However, if you feel comfortable giving it a try, please feel free to do so. Try not to invert wordings to fit a rhyme in but rather strive to find a melodic rhyme (even a slant rhyme).

Can you include any irony? Try to do so.

Imagine the place you are writing about and jot down a series of images about it. Start with a strong image that surprises and intrigues the reader.

Do not use "I" but instead, like Wilbur, use third person. Let this speaker describe in the subsequent tercets nature. What happened in this place? How was the landscape harmed or ruined? How does it look now? Maybe your chosen spot is a childhood home that has now gone to ruin; maybe your poem is about a house in the neighborhood that has fallen to ruin and now the plants and wild things have overtaken it.

Remember to learn from Wilbur about careful and deliberate word choice, particularly verb choice. Do not let adjectives or adverbs tell the story; let the well-chosen action verbs, imagistic verbs, tell the tale. Remember that each word you choose creates tone and affects the reader. Know what tone you want to create, and choose words that convey and create that tone. Consider the connotation of words selected. Words have both literal and interpretative meanings and associations.

Is there a person or are there people in your poem? Paint them in with details as the poem moves down the page. What do they say to one another or think to themselves? How does that contribute to your poem's meaning?

As always, after the first draft, let the poem sit for a while. Come back to it to edit and revise lines, words, and phrases. Share it with your group. Ask what tone or tones are conveyed in your poem. Ask which of your imagery is fresh and meaningful and which just doesn't work or is simply too banal to be effective (something others have heard before).

SAMPLE STUDENT POEMS

Glass Earth

by Ethan Marcus Goode

Manhattan smog clouds shutter the sunrise,
the Pacific chokes on its diet of refuse,
a polar bear drowns in the melted Arctic,
while mankind sits on his crumbling throne
and smiles at the breaking of the world.

Northern Winters

by Tricia Windowmaker

A fresh smell blows upon the wind
Moisture touches your skin

Snowflakes fall;
The night air crawls

The stars begin to spin
And then you see

Colors dance to notes from songs
That softly play in tune.

Accolade to the Morning

by Lacey Hudspeth

Darkness overbears the horizon
While mist holds longingly to the tips of the grass.
Mandolin plays a soft ballad background
Gently plucking the notes of
A crescendo to morning.

Darkness begins to lessen its grip.

Clouds resemble cider down
Blowing sweetly this way and that.
Sink back into my rocking chair
While my coffee blows whiffs of cinnamon and hazelnut
And warms my chest as it settles there.

What playful darkness . . .

A game of cat and mouse with the dawn.
I inhale—preparation for another day.
Tranquility shakes my hand—
Signing a peace treaty to the war.

Darkness crawls into a hole.
Dawn captures the mouse again.

The rising of the sun.
The trajectory of life.

NOTE

Chapter Four

Metaphors and Symbols

Finding and Using Creative Analogies

> Poetry has enriched my life in many ways, but perhaps most by helping me see what I call the Marvelous Connections.
>
> —(Kooser 2005, 140)

Creative analogies are called metaphors, and metaphors offer poets a unique and remarkable opportunity to convey meaning and create strong imagery. A common metaphor is an obvious one: for example, "fame is a bee" by Emily Dickinson. Similes are clear, strong tools used to compare two things by using the words *like* or *as*; Metaphors in general compare two quite different things using creative analogy.

For the simile—my husband is *like a bear*, but for the metaphor—*my husband is a bear*. See the difference? It is subtle but powerful. Sometimes it is better to choose a metaphor; sometimes a simile, an obvious comparison, works better in a given poem and poetic situation.

American Poet Laureate Ted Kooser in his book *The Poetry Home Repair Manual* says that metaphors are confident and definitive, whereas similes are more diffident: For example, what if a poem expressed this line: "The lover hovered like a waiter." The line suggests *that maybe* he acted like a waiter. He was waiter-like. In contrast, "The lover was a waiter, anticipating her next move" is unarguable; it contains no maybe. A serious distinction exists between the two (Kooser 2005, 126).

The metaphor may be stronger than the simile because the simile is an obvious comparison using *like* or *as*, whereas the metaphor is an implied comparison requiring thought and imagination by the reader. The metaphor is more sophisticated; it requires a dialogue with the reader.

The important thing to remember is to be conscious about it. Would a metaphor work better? Or is there some emotional wavering about the comparison, some diffidence that would be better illustrated by the use of simile? However, the tools can be equally effective when used strategically in a poem.

Here too we will introduce two poetic devices: synecdoche and its twin, metonymy. These devices suggest one thing is another or one thing represents another. They are a type of symbolism where one thing stands for the whole or a phrase stands for a well-known thing. Though the two terms have been taught as separate, we suggest using the single term *synecdoche* (sin–*eck*–da–key) for both.

Most books try to define these puzzling devices with the obvious "the pen is mightier than the sword" or "all hands on deck" phrasings. Readers will see how the pen and the sword stand for or represent other things: *the pen* stands for the power of the written word whereas *the sword* represents the act of physical warfare, for instance.

These clever, sophisticated, and useful devices exemplified in such poems as "The Death of the Ball Turret Gunner" by Randall Jarrell or in E. A. Robinson's "Richard Cory" are effective tools of the poetic craft. In the Jarrell poem, the speaker is a dead young soldier in World War II; he tells his story by using examples like these:

"From my mother's *sleep*, I fell into the *State*." "Sleep" represents or stands for the helpless, powerless, and ironically safe place of a child in utero and the relatively safe environment of childhood itself; the State, in this poem, stands for the government, for conscription of young men into war, where they are also powerless but in a perpetual "state" of deadly danger.

Another example is Edwin Arlington Robinson's poem "Richard Cory" (about a wealthy businessman everyone in town admires who one night inexplicably shoots himself) that uses lots of synecdoche: "On we worked and waited for *the light*. / We went without *the meat* and cursed *the bread*."

Note how in both poems, these words are symbolic, even, we could say, symbolic-type metaphors, of other *things*. In "Richard Cory," the light, meat, and bread stand for other things: better days, better pay, more work, improved conditions (the light), the lack of decent food, the poor-quality food, the poverty of a time period in a worker's life (the bread vis-à-vis the meat). It is entirely acceptable to use synecdoche as the inclusive term.

What is the value of such comparisons and symbols? Readers can see how language is in itself the art form, the vehicle of meaning. Metaphors and symbols are creative analogies; they work as some of the best paintbrushes of craft for poets. Watch for them; see how they work to create imagery that delivers emotion, experience, situation, and meaning.

TERMS USED IN THIS CHAPTER

Fixed Forms: Poems that employ some kind of meter, rhyme, rhythm, or line and stanza style. The fixed form can range from the simple couplet (two lines) or tercet (three lines) to the elegant sestina or villanelle. (More on fixed forms in chapter 15.)

Free Forms: Poems without any obvious construction or use of meter, rhyme, or line and stanza style. Nonetheless, even free-form poems have an ear for the musicality of language or rhythm.

Quatrain: Four lines of poetry in a stanza, rhymed or unrhymed.

Synecdoche (and Metonymy): The aristocrat of poetic terms, synecdoche is a symbolic and layered substitution—similar to metaphor—where one thing stands for another or an image or word or phrase stands for meaning on several levels. This book uses *synecdoche* and *metonymy* interchangeably.

Tercets: The three-line stanza used in fixed-form poem such as "The Writer."

THE MODEL POEM

The Writer

by Richard Wilbur

In her room at the prow of the house
Where light breaks, and the windows are tossed with linden,
My daughter is writing a story.

I pause in the stairwell, hearing
From her shut door a commotion of typewriter-keys
Like a chain hauled over a gunwale.

Young as she is, the stuff
Of her life is a great cargo, and some of it heavy:
I wish her a lucky passage.

But now it is she who pauses,
As if to reject my thought and its easy figure.
A stillness greatens, in which

The whole house seems to be thinking,
And then she is at it again with a bunched clamor
Of strokes, and again is silent.

I remember the dazed starling
Which was trapped in that very room, two years ago;
How we stole in, lifted a sash

And retreated, not to affright it;
And how for a helpless hour, through the crack of the door,
We watched the sleek, wild, dark

And iridescent creature
Batter against the brilliance, drop like a glove
To the hard floor, or the desk-top.

And wait then, humped and bloody,
For the wits to try it again; and how our spirits
Rose when, suddenly sure,

It lifted off from a chair-back,
Beating a smooth course for the right window
And clearing the sill of the world.

It is always a matter, my darling,
Of life or death, as I had forgotten. I wish
What I wished you before, but harder.

THE EXPLICATION

"The Writer" offers two stories, a story within a story, one might say. It works through the use of two quite different metaphors, a daughter compared to a trapped starling and a room compared to a ship (of life).

Similes and metaphors (relatively the same thing with the metaphor more deft, more sure) help readers understand what a poet means. Think how a good teacher will often offer a striking analogy to make students understand and master a learning concept. A metaphor is a creative analogy. It's that simple and that powerful.

The reader enters the poem through the image of a daughter "in her room at the prow of the house / Where light breaks, and the windows are tossed with linden," where she is "writing a story." The writer in this poem, the speaker's daughter, works in the "prow of the house." This metaphor of the room compared to a ship's prow suggests that the "writer" travels on some kind of life journey, and on this journey "light breaks"; suggests phrasing shows light coming on inside the mind and light breaking through into one's inner world, the subconscious.

In stanza 2, note the sound imagery. The speaker pauses in the stairwell to listen to the sounds coming from his daughter's "shut door." Apparently this young writer types on an old typewriter, because the poem shares the sound of the "commotion of typewriter-keys / Like a chain hauled over a gunwale."

The poet *extends the metaphor* with a simile "Like a chain hauled . . ." down through another stanza, reinforcing the notion that this daughter's life relates to a ship's journey. The sound, when compared to the commotion of the typewriter keys, becomes much larger than in real life. Wilbur suggests, then, this is a significant time, a momentous time.

Such is the function of the simile, to compare one thing to another in such a way as to add life to the original item, and to stir the reader's emotions. The more common simile needs no explanation; all readers understand the comparison with the use of the words *like* or *as* making the analogy obvious. In contrast, the metaphor is a bit more sophisticated, demanding the reader call up an image.

The reader must participate more fully in metaphor. Poets must create apt and careful metaphors and also decide when and where to use metaphor or simile. It should be a deliberate and thoughtful choice.

Now the speaker goes on to suggest that "young as she is, the stuff / Of her life is a great cargo, and some of it heavy: / I wish her a lucky passage." The ship metaphor has become a poetic conceit, as it now seems to control the entire poem. The business of her life becomes a "great cargo," cargo that at times becomes very "heavy," and for this reason the father wishes "her a lucky passage." Note how the poet sustains his metaphor.

At this point, the speaker notices "it is she who pauses" to think about her life, "as if to reject" his "thought and its easy figure. A stillness greatens. . . ." Note how the poet alters an adjective and makes it a verb! *"Greatens."* How well that works. The speaker has paused in the stairwell. Now his daughter pauses in her room; time seems to stop. The reader stands poised between action and inaction, waiting for more.

From here, the speaker suggests that "the whole house seems to be thinking, / And then she types again with a bunched clamor / Of strokes, and again is silent." Once again the typewriter keys are loud, in this case a *clamor*, reinforcing her youthful life as busy and boisterous.

Note how the poet also trusts the silence to speak; and the silence is another way to communicate with the reader. *What happens and what does not happen, what one hears and what one does not hear are all relevant in a given poem.* What a poet includes and what he or she leaves out is deeply important in any poem. Wilbur proves this in his tender poem. These are all choices a poet makes.

Now the poem makes a dramatic turn and leaves the extended metaphor of the ship behind, opening the door into a new story. To add yet one more descriptive way of looking at the same situation is both clever and inviting. It invites the reader to consider the theme from more than one position.

There is the story of the daughter's journey in the prow of the ship of life, and now the "dazed starling" must find the window to freedom on its journey of freedom, a journey both terrifying and wondrous.

The stanza begins with the father remembering "the dazed starling / Which was trapped in that very room, two years ago; / How we stole in, lifted a sash / And retreated, not to affright it; . . ." The last line here is from the next stanza, but is needed here to continue the stream of thought. Here a "dazed starling" has somehow made its way into this room at the top of the stair and now tries desperately to find its way out into the world.

The speaker has *stolen* into the room and lifted a window in order to offer the bird its freedom. He compares this action to a parent opening the window of life to a child and setting the child free. Even so, finding this small exit proves not to be an easy task for the starling. Neither the bird nor the daughter can easily pass out of this room into the larger world outside.

Continuing in the next stanza, the speaker describes how "for a helpless hour, through the crack of the door, / We watched the sleek, wild, dark / And iridescent creature / Batter against the brilliance, drop like a glove / To the hard floor, or the desk-top." Both the father and the daughter are watching this lovely bird struggling to escape back into the world over and over again without success.

And now they are all waiting, the father and daughter as they peek through the door, the bird as it lay "humped and bloody" on the floor, "for the wits to try it again"; and then their spirits rise when, "suddenly sure, / It lifted off from a chair-back, / Beating a smooth course for the right window / And clearing the sill of the world." The father knows that life may very well leave his daughter "humped and bloody" at times, and the daughter realizes that life will be a difficult struggle.

However, both also know that it will take rising above the difficulties, picking oneself off the floor, and trying once again. And when this is true, when one does climb back up off the floor and try again, at some point, that journey will become clear and sure, the path will open up, and the person will know in which direction to go. When this occurs, both the father and daughter know that the journey into the world will be sure-footed and safe just *like* the suddenly freed starling.

Wilbur's optimistic view of life's journey is evident here in his phrasing about how we must find the right window to "clear the sill of the world." As he did in "First Snow in Alsace," the poet offers a sense of the miraculous in life as well as a hopeful, positive vision of the world. Poets' worldviews are evident in their work. Remember this.

Wilbur ends the poem with a final stanza that has the father once again thinking and in essence talking silently in his mind to his daughter. "It is always a matter, my darling, / Of life or death, as I had forgotten. I wish / What I wished you before, but harder." This memory of the starling battering its way out of the same room where the daughter writes a story reminds the father that living is dangerous; therefore, he wishes her a lucky passage, but he wishes it *harder*, recognizing and imagining as he does the danger.

The poem begins with the father listening and thinking about his daughter while standing in the stairwell; the story continues as the father remembers the incident with the starling two years before, and then ends with the father once again thinking about his daughter in that same stairwell. In truth, this entire poem occurred in just a few moments of the father's life. Poets can learn from this how to frame incidents in poetry.

More importantly perhaps, the poem offers a view of parenting, of youth on the brink of coming of age, of the dangers and miracles of life. We are all writers of our own lives. The poem offers the student of poetry an excellent example of metaphors, of the extended metaphor, of similes, and also of images.

EXERCISES FOR STUDENTS

Quick Exercise 1. Coming up with Metaphors and Similes (15 minutes)

Your task is to create some metaphors and similes that might be useful in a poem. Think about a person you know and what that person *is like*. Come up with a metaphor for the person or the person's situation. (If you prefer to think of a place and find a metaphor for it, that will work too.) Brainstorm a list of at least five metaphors. Change the metaphors to similes. Consider the subtle differences between them. Share these phrases with the class or a writing partner at the end of fifteen minutes.

Quick Exercise 2. Brainstorm a Memory about the Person in Exercise 1 above (15 minutes)

Expand the ideas begun in exercise 1 into the beginnings of a poem. Do this by focusing on one particular memory about the person you have chosen (or the place). Consider thinking of a poetic conceit that would illustrate that person's predicament or situation; express the predicament or situation in a title like the title of Wilbur's poem, so the reader knows from the beginning a metaphor is at work in this poem to be. Share your titles with your group.

THE MODEL EXERCISE

Your assignment is to create a poem that uses an extended metaphor to convey the truth about a person or a place. Remember all that's been learned from the two Wilbur poems about sound, imagery, metaphor/ simile, titles, and structure. Keeping those things in mind and the concept that poets show their worldviews in their art, in their work, spend some quality time just thinking about your person/situation/metaphor. Ask yourself some questions about that person's life story—what did he or she really want? Did he or she achieve that? Or if you wrote about place, how did the place affect the way you saw the world? How did it do that?

What imagery begins to develop in your mind? Put it down on the page in lines now. You might try writing in rhymed or unrhymed tercets, but any form and structure is all right. The focus is on the metaphor itself and memory.

Now go back through the Wilbur poem and highlight the verb choices such as *stole, lifted, trapped, retreated.* Make sure your verbs will be strong and fresh, expressing motion and creating imagery.

Write the poem beginning with the title you selected in exercise 2. The trick is to discover where it starts and ends; this will always be the trick, even when poets are accomplished. Some good advice is to lay down the first image you see in your mind: sight, sound, smell, taste—whatever, start with an image. End with one too, sometimes, even often. Once the first image is on the page, the poem will start talking to you.

Listen to what it says and lay down the lines. Do so without much editing in your head; write them rapidly. Later, go back and filter out the best ones; be ruthless and "kill your darlings," as we say in class. We all hate to delete our own words, but as a poet, one must learn to cut out useless or average or redundant words, images, and phrases ruthlessly.

Free yourself to put all the words on the page for the first draft. In subsequent drafts, you can pick and choose, cull and shine words and phrases and imagery. Once the poem is on the page, let it sit for a while, a day or two or three. Then go back and become your own editor. Read it as if it is someone else's poem. Is the title a metaphor or a hint at metaphor? Does a metaphor control the poem? Is the metaphor fresh and meaningful?

How do the lines look on the page? Work on polishing the line endings. Each line should complete its image for the most part, but on the other hand, sometimes we want the reader to push past the end of the line and keep reading—fast—like a quickly beating heart. If so, you can if you are thoughtful break up the image and wrap the line around, using thoughtful enjambment. How many stanzas? Do you need stanzas? How long are the lines? How does the poem look on the page? Most importantly, did you succeed in creating an extended metaphor that conveys a truth about a person or place? Do strong verbs inhabit that poem?

Spend some time reflecting on all you have learned from Wilbur in the past two chapters. Build on this as a poet. Share your poem with others in class and out.

SAMPLE STUDENT POEMS

Grandmother's Coffee, Black

by E. A. Weatherly

Every morning was the same,
she read her black and white news
with her coffee black.
Sipped from her creamed
and chipped cup of steamed
bitterness—so unlike her.

Delta Freedom

by Chris Shaber

Keys to freedom clutched in his hand.
Walking towards the maroon rocket.
Solid *thunk* as the door closes upon
his childhood. Cool vinyl against his back.
A slight jingling as he awakens the throaty
beast. Hum of static and noise in his ears
until it all becomes clear. Billowing dust,
a temporary signpost of his journey.

Bea and Her Bundle

by Abby Musselman

Flour dipped hands pulled taut cotton dresses
and dreams washed in early morning light.
Rays set fire to crimson leaves dancing
above my head as I sway. The tree groaned

at my annoyance. Red curls placed perfectly
in a mess to shade her blue eyes—eye mirrored
ten feet and two generations away. So determined
to capture the wild sun in her second load of clothes.

The whites. Bleach swirled with Georgia morning
peaches. Just beyond the train tracks every Sunday.
Do not worry, bumble bee, she flashed, we will finish
before the high noon train can ruin them.

NOTES

REFERENCE

Kooser, Ted. *The Poetry Home Repair Manual: Practical Advice for Beginning Poets*. Lincoln: University of Nebraska Press, 2005.

Chapter Five

Line Endings, Turns, and Epiphanies

More Essential Elements of Craft

Always, at the end of each line there exists—inevitably—a brief pause.
This pause is part of the motion of the poem, as hesitation is part of
the dance.

—Mary Oliver, from *A Poetry Handbook* (Oliver 1994, 54)

This chapter will examine another James Wright poem to explore additional useful elements of craft including line endings, turns, and epiphanies. This chapter continues to review and reinforce terms learned and used in previous chapters.

In order to classify a poem as a strong poem, a work must blend seamlessly, magically it seems, the elements of craft and art. No formula exists, per se, and some poets are no doubt more deliberate while others "wing it," using tools that are learned so well they are used intuitively. It is through a poet's mastery of elements of craft coupled with insight and aesthetic taste that we find genius.

To understand and master elements of craft fully as we pursue *art*, we can examine poems word by word, image by image, line by line. In order to fully appreciate craft, readers and aspiring poets must examine poems for more than meaning. That is not to say meaning is not significant and the essence of a poem. Of course it is. It may be the most important thing. But craft is in the building of the poem from the bottom up or more accurately from the top of the page down. It is how the poem works to create meaning.

In this chapter, readers and writers can learn some relevant things about the relationship between how a poem looks and works on the page and how the very shape of a poem controls readers, about how line endings influence pace and meaning, and about how many poems discover their own often-surprising connections and truths.

In *A Poetry Handbook*, Mary Oliver advises poets that

> The pattern on the page, then, became the indicator of pace, and the balance and poise of the poem was inseparable from the way the line breaks kept or failed a necessary feeling of integrity, a holding together of the poem from beginning to end. (Oliver 1994, 56)

In this chapter, we will pay particular attention to the line endings, turns of meaning and surprises midpoem, moments where the speaker experiences a sudden recognition or awareness, an epiphany that illuminates a new thought and offers fresh insight. Wright is a master of such elements of craft.

TERMS USED IN THIS CHAPTER

Epiphany: As in the biblical term, a poetic epiphany means a moment of awakening in which the speaker recognizes some previously hidden truth and is thereby changed in some significant manner if only in understanding. Epiphany is crucial in strong poems, but it must be used with care and should not become didactic. Ideally, epiphany should be or should seem fresh and honest, as if poet and reader discover it at the same time.

Line Endings: Line endings have been mentioned and discussed in the previous chapters, but this chapter focuses on their importance. In poetry as in musical lyrics, line endings are important, and the handling of them with care and deliberation is integral to effective writing. A line can end at a period or comma, or it can "enjamb" into the next line, forcing the reader on. In contrast, a line can end or pause completely at midline—a surprise, a stop time, called a caesura.

In general, students of poetry and emerging writers should beware of keeping their images "whole" on one line while at the same time leading the reader on and controlling the pace and meaning of the poem with apt punctuation or no punctuation in some cases. White space counts in poetry as sound or pause or turn just as white space counts in journalism as space used. The line endings work to control pace; pace works toward tone. Tone works toward meaning.

Point of View: As in fiction and nonfiction prose, point of view refers to the selection of a speaker's diction and attitude. Speakers like narrators select and sustain (usually) one point of view throughout a poem, that of first person, second person, or third person. Each should be used consciously and deliberately with regard to content and intent.

Turns: In classical poetry and that of the sonneteers both Italian and Elizabethan, the turn occurred at the eighth line, where the poem changed from the statement of circumstance to the subsequent action or condition of being. This turn was called a volte by Italian sonnet writers. It is the moment therefore in any poem where the movement and meaning shift to some new condition or recognition. It is at this point that a reader is often surprised and that a deft poet leaps from concrete to abstract meaning.

THE MODEL POEM

A Blessing

by James Wright

Just off the highway to Rochester, Minnesota,
Twilight bounds softly forth on the grass.
And the eyes of those two Indian ponies
Darken with kindness.
They have come gladly out of the willows
To welcome my friend and me.
We step over the barbed wire into the pasture
Where they have been grazing all day, alone.
They ripple tensely, they can hardly contain their happiness
That we have come.
They bow shyly as wet swans. They love each other.
There is no loneliness like theirs.
At home once more,
They begin munching the young tufts of spring in the darkness.

I would like to hold the slenderer one in my arms,
For she has walked over to me
And nuzzled my left hand.
She is black and white,
Her mane falls wild on her forehead,
And the light breeze moves me to caress her long ear
That is delicate as the skin over a girl's wrist.
Suddenly I realize
That if I stepped out of my body I would break
Into blossom.

THE EXPLICATION

James Wright's poem begins with the title "A Blessing" and shows readers the importance of a well-chosen title. Wright's title suggests the reader watch for a blessing in the poem. Recognizing title importance will make for better reading (and better writing! See chapter 12 for more information on this topic).

The reader enters the poem through the line "Just off the highway to Rochester, Minnesota. . . ." This focus on the proper nouns of place can be used to lend verisimilitude to poems. Sometimes it works effectively to do so, whereas at other times, when poorly placed or used too often, specific nouns might just be in the way. It takes sensibility to discern the difference.

Wright stops time and places readers right in the moment by offering a close-up image: through the "eyes of those two Indian ponies," which "Darken with kindness." Note the poetic sensibility of such a moment, the poet's ability to see the miraculous in the mundane, to witness something important in another living creature.

The poem deepens with meaning with this introduction of the animal world, the natural world, into the poem. The personification of twilight bounding softly over the grass suggests one view of the natural world, but to add two young ponies brings the poem alive. In fact, the kindness the speaker witnesses in their eyes causes him to make an assumption about the ponies: "They have come gladly out of the willows / To welcome my friend and me." He *layers his images*, moving from the kind eyes of the ponies to the ponies welcoming of the human strangers.

In the next line, Wright brings the speaker and his friend even closer to the ponies by having them "step over the barbed wire into the pasture" where the two ponies "have been grazing all day, alone." Wright accentuates the word "alone" by placing it behind a comma at the end of the line, so the word stands out. The reader feels a loneliness in the tone of this poem.

In the lines "They ripple tensely, they can hardly contain their happiness / That we have come. / They bow shyly as wet swans. They love each other." It's a remarkable image and simile, one that is tactile ("ripple tensely"—if readers know horses, they will have noticed how the horse's coat ripples to the touch) and one that is surprising, as horses are compared to "wet swans." The horses are shy and seem to bow to the humans who have stopped to commune with them in this lonely field.

Wright accentuates the fact that the ponies have been alone all day. These animals are lonely in their natural world, in the pasture, munching on grass. The appearance of two humans makes them happy and shy both at the same time. The added surprising line "They love each other" causes the reader to pause and notice the progression in the poem from feeling alone in their natural habitat with each other to being exposed to the human world. This becomes an interesting juxtaposition mainly because the very next line says "There is no loneliness like theirs." What does the poet mean? No loneliness like theirs?

Note the control of the poem line by line with the juxtaposition of short and longer lines, the confidence to use caesura and enjambment almost musically. Here is an example of enjambment:

> They have come gladly out of the willows
> To welcome my friend and me.

Notice too the line endings that become powerful because they are carefully chosen:

> Suddenly I realize
> That if I stepped out of my body I would break
> Into blossom.

The word "realize" comes at the moment of epiphany for the speaker/ poet: It is like a diving board at the end of that line. The word "break" at the line's end literally breaks the line in two. Such attention to detail is part of a poet's skill and art.

The speaker continues, "At home once more, / They begin munching the young tufts of spring in the darkness." Somehow darkness hides in the lines of these seemingly ordinary images of ponies and pastures. At this point, the reader waits for something more to come in the next few lines that will help explain this.

The poem takes a hard turn. The reader sees ponies munching grass, when suddenly the reader is thrust into the speaker's mind. He says to himself, "I would like to hold the slenderer one in my arms, / For she has walked over to me / And nuzzled my left hand." Readers will note the surrealist leap of this moment in the poem, the shift from ordinary to extraordinary perception. The imagery, the tone, the lines, the chosen words, suggest a shared loneliness and need for comfort and love, a need shared by both humans and animals.

The poem complements this concept with a concrete description of this female pony: "She is black and white, / Her mane falls wild on her forehead. . . ." Again the poem has referred to the feminine, but also the masculine, the black and the white, the yin and the yang, the sun and the moon, all those symbols that represent both sides of human nature as well as both sides of the universe: darkness and light, male and female, natural and human.

And according to Wright, something wild exists essentially in this combination of opposites. He implies humans and horses are both tame and wild, lonely and independent. In this very moment Wright brings the poem to its conclusion: "Suddenly I realize / That if I stepped out of my body I would break / Into blossom." Look at the joy contained in these last three lines. The speaker has an epiphany, a moment of awakening and new awareness that were he to step out of his body, he would break into blossom because he feels such joy.

Something magical and inexplicable has happened here in this lonely pasture outside Rochester, Minnesota. All the above references to dark/ light, male/female, yin/yang, sun/moon come to fruition when this speaker realizes that to step outside of the human body suggests blossoming in the next world, the world beyond mere human existence. Perhaps, the speaker implies, the body is just a part of this human world, something we leave behind when we step out of it and blossom in our imaginations.

The artful use of the poetic tools of line endings, turns, and an epiphany work together toward multiple thematic interpretations. Wright shows us all how a moment in a horse pasture can become miraculous, a witnessing of sorts, a blossoming of creativity and love.

EXERCISES FOR STUDENTS

Quick Exercise 1. An Epiphany (15 minutes)

Write one paragraph about an encounter you had with one of nature's animals in which you experienced some kind of new knowledge of the relationship or of life. It does not have to be a hugely important moment, yet if you remember it, you will see it was indeed meaningful for some reason.

What did you learn from this interaction? What insight did you gain? This could be a wild animal or a tame one. You can use your own pet if you like. Choose one moment to focus on, and as you write, think about what this moment exemplified to you. Put what this moment meant in the final line. Strive to write five to ten strong lines rich with description and detail.

Quick Exercise 2. Line Endings (15 minutes)

Now, using the paragraph you wrote in exercise 1, edit the prose to find the strongest details and description. Notice that with those details and description, you have created imagery. Delete any obvious or clichéd words, phrases, or images. Leave only the strongest, most effective imagery. Then reline your paragraph into a poem.

Consider how it looks on the page; note the difference between the paragraph of prose and the words as they become a poem. Avoid leaving any odd words at the ends of lines. Use punctuation at the ends of lines unless you want the reader to keep reading through to the next line.

THE MODEL EXERCISE

What can we learn from this Wright poem? It is magical and surreal in many aspects; it leaps from concrete to abstract with such aplomb. This poem teaches us to be fearless in focusing on a physical and actual event but daring enough to leap from it into the wondrous air of imagination and figurative connections.

Begin with an event such as a meeting you have with a wild creature or an animal or animals you rarely see. Start with a specific location for the first line of your poem, something like "Just off the highway to Rochester, Minnesota. . . . " It places the reader in space and time; it confirms the poem's validity. Next, offer an image that shows readers where you are. Describe the approach of the animal(s) as Wright does, by showing their movement from one spot to another. What is your first impression of them? Put it down on the page.

Focus intently on the animals and create some vivid imagery that depicts them. Use the close-up lens of observation; shift your gaze from the wide angle to the macro view. Smells? Touch? Size? Color? Shape? Offer imagery that paints the animals in broad strokes as well as delicate strokes. Let the horse touch your palm, for instance; feel its whiskers and velvet nose. Ask yourself, what is this meeting like? Try to capture the magic in the moment, to feel its grace.

How do you feel at that moment? How are you altered at the moment you and the animals experience a special meeting? What do you think about? How are you transported? Note Wright's final line as he expresses how the moment feels to him.

Wright's poem expresses too what such a brief meeting can mean, an unforgettable meeting that one always remembers. Why is this? Because it felt like a blessing, answers Wright. Think about your own poem this way and title it accordingly.

ALTERNATE MODEL POEM

Skater

by Ted Kooser

She was all in black but for a yellow pony tail
that trailed from her cap, and bright blue gloves

that she held out wide, the feathery fingers spread,
as surely she stepped, click-clack, onto the frozen
top of the world. And there, with a clatter of blades,
she began to braid a loose path that broadened
into a meadow of curls. Across the ice she swooped
and then turned back and, halfway, bent her legs
and leapt into the air the way a crane leaps, blue gloves
lifting her lightly, and turned a snappy half-turn
there in the wind before coming down, arms wide,
skating backward right out of that moment, smiling back
at the woman she'd been just an instant before.

ALTERNATE MODEL EXERCISE

Write a poem about watching someone do something physical. Perhaps you watch your boyfriend play tennis, or you watch your grandmother cook dinner. Pick any specific physical exercise and put it down on the page.

This poem is more pragmatic and less fanciful, one might say, than the previous poem by Wright. Still, it has its own magical metaphors and turns. Note that Mr. Kooser's poem is like a snapshot of mind: The speaker is watching a girl skating. The poem opens with an image full of color and rich details as in "bright blue gloves that she held out wide, the feathery fingers spread." We have sound, "a clatter of blades," and an interesting verb choice, "braid," as the girl skates through "a meadow of curls."

Nine of the thirteen lines in this poem are enjambed, while the others barely slow the pace with commas. The line endings serve the poem: They keep it flowing; they keep it moving like the skater. There are only two caesuras, and each occurs at a moment when the poem makes a turn. In the middle of the poem the girl swoops and leaps, bends her legs "the way a crane leaps" and makes "a snappy half-turn / there in the wind before coming down." A study of this poem shows the power of well-chosen images using color and sound and apt metaphor.

Note the onomatopoeia of "click-clack" and the alliterative "feathery fingers" and "bright blue."

Finally, the poem takes a leap in the final two lines, shifting from the real to the surreal; it is an epiphany of sorts, a revelation that such beautiful motion seems to reshape time or illustrate it. The speaker says the girl smiles "back / at the woman she'd been just an instant before." Indeed. Now that is a fine leap the reader did not anticipate. We can learn from this poem.

Write a poem that finds its situation in your observation of a person performing some action of work or play. It could be something as seemingly mundane as your mother doing the dishes or your child crawling toward a red ball on the floor. It might be an athlete in motion on the basketball court, a dancer in tulle from your dance class. Whatever. Choose your subject; observe. Jot down all images and phrases that occur to you. Make sure you notice color and shape and sound. Be specific.

After you have done that, building on what was learned in chapter 4, find a metaphor for the person's motion. What does that motion or posture remind you of? An animal? What? Create an interesting and apt metaphor that helps readers see the person and understand the situation. Make sure the metaphor serves the poem.

Then think about what this action or behavior calls into your mind about the person. Finally, ask yourself, what does this one person's motion and experience suggest about human existence or other human beings? Save the answer to that leap for your final two lines.

Now working from your list, edit out all obvious and redundant images and details. Save the best ones, the most colorful and evocative. Line by line, begin your poem. Open with the image showing the person observed and the action performed. In this poem, you will pay attention to line endings: Use the enjambed line with aplomb! Make it work for you and sweep your reader, where relevant, round to the next line, controlling the pace. Use at least one full stop or caesura (midline). Make it a deliberate spot.

Try dividing your poem into three parts: the intro, where you simply describe the action using color and sound; the body, where you create one strong metaphor; and the conclusion, where you make a leap of consciousness or express an epiphany you had while observing and thinking.

Lay it down carefully on the page. Make sure you use a little alliteration; let the sounds you create serve the poem's meaning.

SAMPLE STUDENT POEMS

Breathless

by Sandra Scott

Her lungs lay on the floor
full of screams of loss
swollen with the things
she cannot bear to speak
incapable of breathing the sorrows
that choke the chambers
of her ravaged heart
chased by a chemical cure
playing mind games with the devil.

Echoing with emptiness, her chest
heaves hollow words that strain
to create a song of love,
but the resident evil inflicts
a fresh wound
reminding her of the
pain that comes with living.

Starched White[1]

by Peggy Aiello

Starched white covers veil Victoria's frightened,
fragile frame. Her daughter's eyes take in the moment,
searching for clues,
left . . . alone
caring for the patient that resembles her mother.
Downstairs the teapot whispers for her to come
take a cup to the weary. Quiet calm immerses
the room; sweet peace covers
Victoria's face, her pale hand slides slowly
off the bed. She trembles. Fear
of the truth searches out the perfect pillow

for placement under her mother's frail fingers; cradling
them like a kitten, and resting finally. Searching
her eyes, shaded by transparent lids,
for peace.

NOTES

Credit: Ted Kooser, "Skater" from *Delights & Shadows*. Copyright © 2004 by Ted Kooser. Reprinted with the permission of The Permissions Company, Inc. on behalf of Copper Canyon Press, www.coppercanyonpress.org.

Credit: James Wright, "A Blessing" and "Beginning" from *Collected Poems* © 1963 by James Wright. Reprinted by permission of Wesleyan University Press.

1. This poem won the Debra Vazquez Excellence in Poetry Award, 2008, from the Florida Association of Community Colleges Annual Press Conference.

REFERENCE

Oliver, Mary. *A Poetry Handbook: A Prose Guide to Understanding and Writing Poetry*. San Diego, CA: Harcourt Inc., 1994.

Chapter Six

The Speaker and the Reader

A Dialogue

And so there exists a definite sense of a person, a perfectly knowable person, behind the poem.

—Mary Oliver, from *A Poetry Handbook* (Oliver 1994, 79)

Chapters 1 through 5 have offered a number of essential elements of craft as well as a suggestion for how to observe and witness the world as a poet using beyond-the-ordinary sensibilities. We have presented some strong model poems to illustrate these qualities. Each of the model poems had an identifiable if unnamed speaker and a poetic situation that involved what was happening in the poetic landscape (both physical and emotional), where it was happening, and to whom it was happening.

For instance, in Robert Frost's poem "Out, Out" the speaker is someone who has heard about what happened to a young boy working in a carpentry shop whose hand is cut off by a buzz saw and who ultimately, and very quickly, dies. This speaker has a certain quality of omnipotence in his point of view (ability to view the circumstances and characters and know inside truths), as he seems to know how the boy is feeling, how the townspeople feel, how the sister feels. Moreover, this speaker seems to understand the harsh pragmatism of Yankee townspeople as if he too lived among them.

This speaker is someone like Frost himself, no doubt, but he is not Frost. Intrinsically, a separation exists between author/poet and speaker/narrator. The speaker is an artificial creation who, after the witnessing of experience, offers it up on the page. The speaker has a certain attitude; the poet creates the speaker to tell the poem, to lay it down on the page in the most effective fashion.

The moment a reader opens a book of poetry and begins to read a poem, an emotional dialogue begins with the speaker in the poem. This speaker functions like a real person speaking to the reader; sometimes the person is close and personal, and sometimes the person remains distant and cool. The poem does actually move both ways—the speaker speaks and the reader listens and, more often than not, responds in some fashion on an emotional level.

Readers enter a poem through the voice of the speaker and establish something akin to a dialogue between the two. It is on an emotional level. It is from the heart of the reader, the very soul of the reader. If the speaker is losing his wife to cancer, the reader may connect with that kind of grief and loss. It's important to understand the relationship between the speaker's voice and the reader's listening heart.

Speakers are akin to narrators in fiction and prose. While we talk about the speaker rather than the narrator in poems, the poet makes similar choices with her speaker. In fact, regarding speaker, the poet has many choices to make, beginning with which point of view to choose for the speaker: Will it be first person (using *I, we, me, us*); second person (using *you/your*); a combination of first and second; third person (no first person or second person but only objective pronouns *he/she, they/them, her/him,* etc.)?

Poets make that choice based on which point of view would work best to convey the poem's meaning. Consider, for example, if James Wright had used third person instead of the personal, intimate first person in his poem "A Blessing":

> They have come gladly out of the willows
> To welcome *two friends. (instead of "my friend and me.")*

Or imagine the difference of the powerful final lines were they in third person instead of first person:

> And the light breeze moves *him* to caress her long ear
> That is delicate as the skin over a girl's wrist.
> Suddenly he realizes
> That if he stepped out of his body he would break
> Into blossom.

What if the father writing in the first-person *I* in "The Writer" by Richard Wilbur had chosen the second-person point of view instead? It would read like this:

> In *your* room at the prow of the house
> Where light breaks, and the windows are tossed with linden,
> *You* are writing a story.
> *Your* father pauses in the stairwell, hearing
> From *your* shut door a commotion of typewriter-keys
> Like a chain hauled over a gunwale.

See the difference? It's a vast difference that influences the entire poem's effect on readers. This is not to say that one point of view is superior to others, but that the choice of point of view affects the reader's dialogue with the speaker in an integral way. Poets learn to be conscious of and careful with their choices of point of view for their speakers in each individual poem. The use of *I* and *me*, for instance, implies the speaker was the participant in the poem's action, emotion, and circumstance.

The interesting thing to learn here is (a) there are choices to be made regarding which kind of speaker and (b) even if the poet is actually the main person in the poem, even if the action and circumstances happened to the poet himself or herself, that poet can choose to use a different point of view. Sometimes with very emotional material, taking oneself out of the first person is a fine idea. It creates distance in perspective, and that distance offers the poet the ability to view himself or herself in the third person. It offers, one could say, emotional breathing room. And that is really important.

Point of view is not the only choice a poet makes regarding the speaker either; other important choices include the level of language the speaker will use (diction) and the attitude the speaker will take about the poem's situation and toward the reader. How does the chosen speaker use language? Is it folksy and personal? Is it arrogant and haughty? Does the speaker use elevated language? If so, why? And does that choice serve the poem?

Most importantly, perhaps, is the level of honesty the speaker offers. Is the text reliable? Or is there subtext, hinting at darker things, motives, meanings? Tone is the key to these answers, as is a good ear.

THE MODEL POEM

The Whipping

by Robert Hayden

The old woman across the way
is whipping the boy again
and shouting to the neighborhood
her goodness and his wrongs.

Wildly he crashes through elephant ears,
pleads in dusty zinnias,
while she in spite of crippling fat
pursues and corners him.

She strikes and strikes the shrilly circling
boy till the stick breaks
in her hand. His tears are rainy weather
to woundlike memories:

My head gripped in bony vise
of knees, the writhing struggle
to wrench free, the blows, the fear
worse than blows that hateful

Words could bring, the face that I
no longer knew or loved . . .
Well, it is over now, it is over,
and the boy sobs in his room,

And the woman leans muttering against
a tree, exhausted, purged—
avenged in part for lifelong hidings
she has had to bear.

THE EXPLICATION

In "The Whipping" a young boy takes a brutal beating, and the speaker
witnesses; midpoem, the speaker himself begins to talk in the first person

as if he is the boy being beaten or as if he himself remembers his own similar experience. In either case, it's a surprising twist for a speaker to shift from third-person witness to first-person participant and back again in the middle of any poem. Thus from this fine poem by Robert Hayden all poets can learn about point of view and perspective and how these two things affect the reader.

In the beginning, the speaker describes the woman whipping the boy as an "old woman," though the poem does not tell the reader who she is specifically. That's probably a good thing to remember—when to be specific and when to be impersonal and anonymous. Keep it in mind.

Whoever the old woman might be, she whips "the boy again / and shouting to the neighborhood / her goodness and his wrongs." The speaker lets the reader know this woman tries to justify her actions by "shouting to the neighborhood / her goodness and his wrongs." She seems to need and expect the approval of the neighborhood.

Younger readers may be more appalled than older readers who grew up in times when spankings and even beatings like this were not so uncommon (though not less potentially traumatizing).

Hayden organizes the poem into six stanzas of four lines each, a structure that echoes the chaotic movement in the poem itself. He controls the form while the old woman beats the boy "across the way." The boy runs "wildly" away from this woman, "crashes through elephant ears," and "pleads in dusty zinnias."

Note how the poet names the plants in the garden (elephant ear philodendron and zinnias) as if he knows that garden well and has himself stumbled and hidden within those plants. The woman "corners him." They are both "wildly" running through the yard. It's as if traumatic memories are chaotic by nature.

Note the speaker says the old woman pursues the boy "in spite of crippling fat." On a physical level, this woman is obese, yet on a metaphorical level the word "crippling" implies that the old woman's anger has been triggered by whatever this young boy has done wrong. She can't control herself; she is anger's agent. She becomes a tyrant in pursuit of some kind of emotional release through whipping this boy.

This chaos continues as "she strikes and strikes the shrilly circling / boy till the stick breaks / in her hand." Hayden does two things at this point. He ends line 1 with the word "circling," and it's a shrill "circling," so that the reader becomes caught up in the movement in the poem; then he brings the boy back into the poem on the next line, where "the stick breaks / in her hand." He ends the line on the word "breaks," where the reader can almost hear the snap, and ends the line midline with caesura, a period or full stop.

The reader has the "shrilly circling / boy" and the dynamic of the stick breaking as Hayden brings the poem to a full stop.

Now the speaker makes a hard turn in the poem by saying "his tears are rainy weather / to woundlike memories": Note the colon at the end of this wording. It sets the stage for something to now take place that has to do with "woundlike memories." It hearkens the enjambment. Pay attention, reader, it says. It's an important moment in the poem when the speaker shifts into first person. There are two distinct settings, one in the neighbor's yard and the other in the speaker's memory.

Hayden uses alliteration such as the repeated letter *w* that bears an ominous tone (i.e., way, whipping, wildly, weather, writhing, wrench, worse, words, well, and woman twice). This device creates cohesion and seems itself rather wild, echoing the chaos and wildness of the poem's contents and the roads of memory.

The first-person speaker confesses, "My head gripped in bony vise / of knees, the writhing struggle / to wrench free, the blows, the fear / worse than blows that hateful / Words could bring, the face I / no longer knew or loved. . . ." Note that Hayden ends this six-line section of the poem with ellipses, as if this event goes on forever in memory. Although the speaker is now adult, the memory remains "woundlike" even in the present.

More often than not, when a poem or part of a poem suddenly shifts to first person, the reader feels that the story being told comes from a real-life experience. The sudden shift from third to first person, from description of an outside event to narrating a personal experience midpoem without explanation, seems to suggest that in witnessing an act of trauma, his own personal memory of a beating is triggered.

Or it might suggest that the speaker was trying to tell his own story in the third person when the more frank, open, confessional first person thrust through. That's how it works. It teaches all poets to use and choose point of view with great sensibility.

At this point, in the middle of stanza 5, the poem reverts back to third person as if the poet has regained control of himself and his poem. He writes, "Well, it is over now, it is over, / and the boy sobs in his room." Although these lines directly refer to the *boy across the way*, the reader knows they relate back to the speaker's memory too.

The speaker knows he is no longer powerless like the young boy in the neighbor's yard, though the memory still reflects pain. It is as if the two boys become one somehow, two beaten boys, two wounded psyches. Is the child in us ever really gone?

In the final stanza the speaker makes a judgment about what has taken place in the neighbor's yard. The woman now "leans muttering against / a tree, exhausted, purged," exhausted from chasing and whipping the child. But the speaker says she is also "purged," a judgment that suggests there was more going on here than a simple beating of a child by this old, fat woman. The event has left her feeling "purged," and readers wonder from what? From her own anger only? Or from her own awful memories that provoke her current rages? Note the use of the dash after the word "purged":

a tree, exhausted, purged—

What does it suggest?

The speaker ends with one final comment: "avenged in part for lifelong hidings / she has had to bear." The adult speaker recognizes and understands what kind of past is often the driving force behind such abuse. He makes the connection: Those abused become abusers. Not always, of course. Note again, the poet seems to be showing us truths, dark and terrible ones. Here lies the irony. The once-beaten boy is lifted from his powerless despair and the adult from his old wounds of memory by some kind of understanding. This is one mark of fine poetry and great literature in general: the ability to connect with others, a reaching for the highest possible understanding.

We don't know exactly what happened to the poet or whose voice this is in actuality. Listen: What poets should be after is the *emotional truth* of an experience, not the *actual truth*. Poetry is not a venue for revenge or even confessing your sins. But you can use your own experience and draw from it. Of course, in the end, the level of information conveyed is entirely the artist's own choice.

Hayden uses many tools of craft beyond those he uses to create speaker and point-of-view shift. He is a master poet with an eye for structure and an ear for controlling the tone (in this case, a dark tone about childhood abuse). He can *hear his memory*; he can lay it down image by image on the page. Hayden uses specific words, not general wording. He is precise and specific with language. He goes beyond simple word choice to clever handling of diction and the use of sound devices for effect. Most of all it shows us the complexity of point of view and perspective.

EXERCISES FOR STUDENTS

Quick Exercise 1a. Point of View (20 minutes)

In this exercise your major goal is to create a fictitious voice in order to tell the reader a story. Look back to your childhood and try to uncover an event you want to share with the class. To whom do you want to tell the story? A friend, perhaps, who played a part in this event? Or perhaps you want to tell the story from a first-person point of view. You could even retell the event from the mother's point of view, who is looking out the kitchen window. Once you have chosen the speaker, begin to relate your event. Write down four sentences. Go back and see if you can add an image, a smell or color or sound. Be precise and specific with word choices.

Quick Exercise 1b. Alliteration (30 minutes)

Spend fifteen minutes thinking about one incident from your childhood. It does not need to be a bad experience like the beating that takes place in the Hayden poem. It should, nonetheless, be an incident that is memorable for some good reason.

Brainstorm on paper the details of something you witnessed. This could be an event so seemingly simple as a mother shaking a child's arm or hushing a child in public, at a restaurant, at the mall. Or maybe you witnessed a couple breaking up or having an argument, that triggered memories of a personal breakup or argument. It's important you choose a scenario that made you think about your own life experience, bad or good (if possible. If you can't, just describe the incident).

Now brainstorm the images as they come into your mind. Watch your memory as you would watch a film: frame by frame. Put the frames on the page as a list of images. Be specific and detailed. Choose the unusual, not the obvious details. Set the scenario of the poem in a particular setting as Hayden did. Show where the speaker is standing or sitting or listening in reference to the other characters.

Quick Exercise 2. Choosing a Point of View (15 minutes)

From the images generated in exercise 1, write a paragraph about the incident, selecting a third-person observational speaker. Use the most effective and unusual of your images. Set the incident in time and place somehow so that we know the speaker is witnessing the event. Somewhere in the paragraph, shift to the first-person point of view and connect with your own personal memory that was triggered by what you witnessed.

If you can't do this, it's okay. Just stick to the third-observer point of view. Choose a point of view for your speaker: This time when you construct a poem, remember the speaker is a persona, a voice through whom the events will be narrated. The speaker is not "you" in the real world.

THE MODEL EXERCISE

Write a poem based on a specific incident you recall from childhood. It could be something that happened to you or to someone else. It could be a moment when you witnessed something that evoked your own personal memory.

In any case, in this poem you will offer a third-person narrator or speaker. Someplace in the poem—midpoem perhaps—you might try shifting into the first person to share personal emotions, and then shift back to third person. This poem should be an exercise in learning to control point of view. It should also focus on the sound of selected words and phrasings.

Build on the work you have already done in exercises 1 and 2 above. Consider the diction of your poem's speaker. Imagine what kind of language this speaker would use—language like your own? Different? Just think about diction and be aware of it as you make your word choices.

In this poem, think about how the language sounds. Add some alliteration that will not be overdone but will influence the poem's mood and tone. Choose your words not only for meaning but for sound: Remember how Hayden used the repeated *w* consonant as if to repeat *wound wound wound* in the reader's consciousness. Choose a consonant to use and repeat alliteratively for effect; keep in mind your choices will affect the tone and ultimately serve the poem's intent and meaning.

Now take your paragraph and change it into a poem. Put the images on the page in some order. Pay attention to line endings. Use one caesura in a meaningful place; use several enjambments to move readers from line to line. Control the pace of the poem with these devices, but remember you also control the pace of the poem by how the poem looks on the page. How long are the lines? How many lines to a stanza? Try writing in four quatrains as Hayden does.

Here you have a choice: Do you sustain your selected point of view throughout the poem, or do you shift it midpoem, using a punctuation mark to indicate shift, like a colon? It's up to you. Shifting point of view is a tricky thing, but give it a try if you feel confident and brave.

Remember, this shift of point of view is an unusual thing to do in any poem, a very unusual thing; do it here to learn how to control the speaker. Do not overuse this in subsequent poems.

Now go back and polish your poem. Read it aloud to yourself and to others. Edit out all extraneous words. Title it something to do with the action.

SAMPLE STUDENT POEMS

The Mother's Son

by Judy Haisten

The delicately fine cloth caressed his newly born face
as the woman gave him
to the nurse who had promised to bring him right back
before she carried away
the mother's son.

The impossible cowlick swirled across his childish face
as the boy took the hand
of the teacher who had promised to bring him back
before she led away
the mother's son.

The washed out baseball cap angled his youthful face
as the teen sprinted out to the car
of the buddies who had promised to bring him back
before they drove away
the mother's son.

The gentle smile tendered his love struck face
as the groom tucked the arm
of the bride who had promised to bring him back
before the limo whisked away
the mother's son.

The cold prison bars pressed against his troubled face
as the young man looked with watered eyes
at the guard who promised to come right back
and take away
the mother's son.

The Mourning

by Adam J. Roundtree, Sr.

Through the grey haze of clouded past,
I relive the morning.

Rather than weary eyes,
my ears find confusion.
I lift my head for clarity,
but soon repent, regretting what I've found.

I squeeze my eyes tight,
and fight to resurrect my sleep—
trying hard not to hear the sobs
that have replaced the clinking kitchen dishes.

Past my struggle to deafen the sounds,
I hear every word.
In the solitude of my room,
only I know that I share their sorrow.

A trinity of helplessness.

Their fight is one of survival—
of mind and marriage—
but beneath her grief, the war

NOTE

Credit: "The Whipping" Copyright © 1966 by Robert Hayden, from *Collected Poems of Robert Hayden* by Robert Hayden, edited by Frederick Glaysher. Used by permission of Liveright Publishing Corporation.

REFERENCE

Oliver, Mary. *A Poetry Handbook: A Prose Guide to Understanding and Writing Poetry*. San Diego, CA: Harcourt Inc., 1994.

Chapter Seven

Narrative Poetry

Poems That Tell Stories

Not all poems tell stories, but many are narrative, that is, they follow a
sequence of events over a period of time.

—Ted Kooser, from *The Poetry Home Repair Manual*
(Kooser 2005, 81)

To some extent, all poetry tells stories, little stories, even big stories. It is
a dialogue between writer and reader; it is narrative by nature. Certainly
not all poems are little stories, but telling stories in short poems can be
interesting. Narrative poetry has a long tradition in literature. Some of the
earliest poems in world literature are narratives; *Beowulf* is an epic narrative poem, and Chaucer's *Canterbury Tales* comprise a group of narrative
poems.

Narrative means "story." To write in narrative is to tell a story, brief or
long, simple or complex. Many poems, particularly contemporary ones,
are narrative-type poems, if brief narratives; they tell the story of one
particular experience. Narrative can be used in many types of poems;
therefore, it is not necessarily in itself a separate genre, though it can be,
as with the classic works mentioned above. In a sense, every poem is a
little story about the human experience.

What not to do: In fiction, length is not an issue; therefore, writers use
plenty of well-chosen adverbs to show connection and create cohesion.
However, in poetry, length is an issue. This is a good moment to remind
emerging poets to trust the images to speak, to delete any unnecessary
and redundant words, to trust their readers to make leaps of meaning and
consciousness without clumsy adverbs. In short, the best poets avoid the

use of words like *then* and *thus* and *following that*. Poetry is not a news article. It is art.

In the following two model poems, one by Nebraska poet Ted Kooser and the other by Yankee poet Robert Frost, note the absence of such adverbs. Note how the lines move from incident to incident without adverbs or explanation deftly and clearly. Learn from these how poets tell stories in a few lines through well-chosen, surprising, and effective imagery as well as with well-chosen figurative devices.

TERMS USED IN THIS CHAPTER

Litotes or Understatement: The use of understated emotion, the withholding of emotion, in a situation where great emotion is felt and might be expected. The withholding of emotion draws even greater attention to the depth of feeling by its very control.

Narrative: The word *narrative* in poetry is similar to narration in fiction and nonfiction prose in that it means "telling a story." Poems are sometimes narratives of one brief but meaningful event, almost always personal and even intimate in nature.

Synesthesia: This device is a type of imagery as well as a type of metaphor that rests on the artistic mixing of the senses in a unique and fresh way; for example, "the sweet sound of the train's horn pouring softly over her bed."

THE MODEL POEM

Former Poet Laureate Ted Kooser is a genius at metaphor, of asking and answering "what is something like?" and creating from that answer strong images.

He is a down-to-earth writer, using everyday happenings in the small town and rural life of America. Many of his poems are narratives, little stories told in a few lines, often in one stanza.

This poem tells a story about the speaker's relationship to his old dog, and through that brief story, set in a particular time and place, the poet offers a philosophical conclusion about growing old, about dying, about the nature of the human bond with a dog. Note the ambivalence in this poem, the way its tone is both light and dark, darkly meditative yet ecstatic in certain moments. That kind of dramatic tension is the heart of genius. Let's see how Kooser does it.

January 19
Still thawing, breezy

by Ted Kooser

Arthritic and weak, my old dog Hattie
stumbles behind me over the snow.
When I stop, she stops, tipped to one side
like a folding table with one of the legs
not snapped in place. Head bowed, one ear
turned down to the earth as if she
could hear it turning, she is losing the trail
at the end of her fourteenth year.
Now she must follow. Once she could catch
a season running and shake it by the neck
till the leaves fell off, but now they get away,
flashing their tails, as they bound off
over the hill. Maybe she doesn't see them
out of those clouded, wet brown eyes,
maybe she no longer cares. I thought
for a while last summer that I might die
before my dogs, but it seems I was wrong.
She wobbles a little way ahead of me now,
barking her sharp small bark,
then stops and trembles, excited, on point
at the spot that leads out of the world.

THE EXPLICATION

Kooser begins with a title like a postcard to someone in another state where the weather might be a little warmer. This begins as a postcard of human experience, offering a narrative, brief and powerful. He even adds a specific date. The title itself becomes ironic and surprising after the reader enters the poem. The speaker uses his walk with his old dog, Hattie, to share an insight into aging and dying. Readers will see how Kooser uses a dark monotone that both keeps his poem from growing sentimental and presages its deeper meaning.

After reading the title, the reader enters the poem through the image of the dog: "Arthritic and weak, my old dog Hattie / stumbles behind me over the snow." Already the reader becomes aware that this dog probably has seen its better days and now it "stumbles" over the snow instead of at full speed ahead. Note the importance of the carefully chosen verb. Readers feel sympathy for Hattie and imagine her legs weak and wobbly. Kooser nudges sentiment but does not cross into sentimentality.

He describes the dog in great detail, continuing by saying: "When I stop, she stops, tipped to one side / like a folding table with one of the legs / not snapped in place." His wonderful comparison of his dog leaning to one side like a table not quite snapped into place, calls up a sense of compassion for this dog in the reader. It is a surprising and powerful metaphor. It is unexpected. Now Kooser adds yet one more image. "Head bowed, one ear / turned down to the earth as if she / could hear it turning, she is losing the trail / at the end of her fourteenth year."

At fourteen, his dog nudges so close to the beyond that it is as if she can even hear her own end coming. She has lost the trail (of life, both literally and figuratively), the ability to smell the scent on nature's trails. Ironically, now she can hear what no dog can possibly hear. The speaker says, "Now she must follow." This is a volte of sorts, a turn where we are moved not just from the old dog to the dying dog, not just from the here to the hereafter, but also from the actual to the extraordinary perception.

How does he make that turn? For one thing, Kooser employs caesura with the period in midline. Note how the reader stops short.

> Now she must follow. Once she could catch
> a season running and shake it by the neck
> till the leaves fell off, but now they get away,
> flashing their tails, as they bound off
> over the hill.

The use of caesura pulls the reader up short, makes the reader focus deeply on that moment and that image. So weak and arthritic, the old dog no longer can lead in this world, yet she can do a rather magical thing (note the use of the surreal perception on the poet's part) and place her ear down to the ground to hear the next world. It is as if she begins to chase death now rather than rabbits.

The speaker looks back on all the things the dog used to do: "Once she could catch / a season running and shake it by the neck / until the leaves fell off. . . ." The speaker seems proud when he describes her strong and agile body as it was in youth; similarly, he expresses a melancholy about her decline. But this poet never tells readers how he feels; he never tells readers how to feel. *He lets the images tell, one by one.*

After describing what she could do once, Kooser describes what she can do no longer: "but now they get away, / flashing their tails, as they bound off / over the hill." The poet has a way of taking the sting out of what his dog has lost by using images of what he sees in his own mind's eye, a symbolic "seeing" (just as Wright does), a surreal type of vision. The monotone is a kind of litotes, an understatement of feeling. Litotes controls sentimentality. Kooser finds just the right images to keep the poem from being sentimental and to make the loss of this old dog more bearable for the reader and the writer as well.

The speaker goes on in a hopeful tone, saying that "maybe she doesn't see them / out of those clouded, wet brown eyes, / maybe she no longer cares." Note the delicate interplay of light and dark, hope and despair, death and life. This ability to weave opposite emotions in one poem can be a poet's gift.

And now Kooser makes a major turn in his poem similar to Wright's turn in "A Blessing": "I thought / for a while last summer that I might die / before my dogs, but it seems I was wrong." All of a sudden, we see the speaker is also thinking about his own aging and his own approaching death. Now the poem has become larger in scope. We see the dog and the man's relationship to the dog is symbolic of life's journey. It's a critical turn in the poem, lifting it above the common and into the philosophical, the spiritual.

The poem says Hattie "wobbles a little way ahead of me now, / barking her sharp small bark, / then stops and trembles, excited, on point / at the spot that leads out of the world." The dog is showing her human the way out of the world too, just as she has been his fine companion on earth. It's an extraordinary notion, indeed.

The speaker begins to face the loss of his dog. She "barks her small bark" and "trembles, excited" though she faces death. Kooser suggests the old hunting dog still points the way for her master and the way now is toward death.

Let's look at signal words, primarily adverbs. In common speech and in literary prose, writers use many well-chosen adverbs to signal change, feeling, connection, difference. The common words include *then*, *after*, and *next* as the most often used; of course, more sophisticated adverbs like *nevertheless*, *nonetheless*, *consequently*, and *therefore* also are common signal words. The point is, poetry is no place for them. In poetry, we want the images to make the connections and the reader to find her own way without signposts. Adverbs can be both intrusive and editorial; they tell readers what to do and what to think. Note how Kooser uses none in his poem. He does use the word *now* twice (oddly enough) and the conjunction *but* once. Other than that, the imagery hangs together just fine. The reader moves with the speaker and the dog. The point is, get the common adverbs and most signal words out of poetry. Watch out for the word *then*, particularly in narrative writing.

Kooser uses many craft techniques to write this fine short narrative poem. Strong and concrete images of this aging dog, a major turn, well-chosen words, control of tone, enjambment and caesura, and the leap at the end all blend masterfully to create this poem.

EXERCISES FOR STUDENTS

Quick Exercise 1. Think of a Story Worth Telling (15 minutes)

Note: For this exercise, choose a photo of you and a pet or an animal.

Use your photograph to inspire you in this exercise and the poem to follow. Brainstorm an incident about a pet you have owned who has grown old or has died. Just let your thoughts flow in a list of details or imagery on the page. Using Kooser's poem as your impetus, of course, set your narrative in time and place. Make sure your images are rich with concrete details and description. Ask yourself, why was this a meaningful experience? What does it show to me? What might it convey to readers? Write that down as one sentence.

Quick Exercise 2. Pruning and Culling (20 minutes)

Using your list of details and images above, cull any words that are prose-like, such as *then*, *next*, or *after*. Just delete them and note how your poem in progress still makes sense. Poetry readers are good readers; they understand relationships without prompting adverbs. Begin to line your poem, remembering everything learned in previous chapters about line endings, the use of punctuation, enjambment, and caesura. Delete any redundant language or anything sentimental. We can learn from Kooser to be kind and offer the most genteel sensibilities about life and death and human experience but to never be sentimental. It's hard to write about losing a pet without becoming sentimental, but this is your job in the poem, okay?

THE MODEL EXERCISE

Write a poem that uses the Kooser poem as a model, in which you tell a brief story, anecdotally, about your relationship to and experience with a living creature. Choose a particular moment in time, a setting in time and place actual and concrete. Begin the poem with an observation of the concrete details around the poem's place and setting in time.

Kooser's poem ultimately moves beyond the personal to express a larger, universal truth. In your poem, it is your option to strive for that kind of philosophizing or not. Do keep in mind that from your poem, readers will draw truths that resonate with their own experience. A poem is always a dialogue with readers. It is not just your own personal truth.

Model the poem line by line, careful with line breaks, images, and use of caesura and enjambment. Make something "homely" into something miraculous. Begin with an ironic title such as Kooser's that places the reader in time and place yet surprises the reader immediately with the discussion of a truly personal situation rather than the title's postcard-like blitheness.

If you have trouble beginning such a poetic exercise, use the first line from either poem to prompt you. Perhaps you could go through old and treasured photographs at home. Find one or two that show you with a pet. Study the photograph. Brainstorm the concrete images on paper. Continue to think of the moment in time between you and the creature as a photograph in your head; paint it onto the page, image by image.

In the first few lines, place the poem in space and time (look at that photo! When, where? Sensory objects and impressions?). Review the first lines of the Kooser poem. Follow his example for setting, for place. Next, use a proper noun to identify the specific pet (it is not just "a" rabbit but Brooks, the specific lop-eared European longhair, for example). Such details help the poem establish veracity and help readers trust the poem.

Then, realize you must decide on the few, polished details and imagery to tell the story. Show the pet, using carefully chosen imagery. Don't tell us what we would see but show us what we would not, what only you see when you look at your beloved pet. Offer up the unexpected images not the expected; avoid redundancy and the commonplace observation.

At the same time, don't be afraid of the simple, clear details to illustrate your story. Do not use the word *then*; in fact, avoid it in general. Poets must be aware of the difference between fiction or prose narrative and the brief, clear details of narrative poetry. You needn't lead readers from line to line; expect them to follow you even in your wild leaps. If your imagery is strong and clear, readers will follow you. Do not explain. Do not use adverbs to show movement. Use verbs. Use nouns turned into verbs.

Somewhere around midpoem or two-thirds of the way through, ask yourself, what do I imagine to be true of this pet and what happened to it? What must it represent to me and to my life? That kind of thinking will lead you to real epiphanies of meaning. Create a turn in the poem there. Did the incident move you to any epiphany, a moment when you learned something important about life bad or good, both maybe, that changed you and your perception of life?

Please let us remind you to be responsible with your imagery. If your pet died in a gruesome accident, do not re-create it on the page so that readers too must suffer it in their minds forever. Don't shirk from the truth of it either. Lay down *the emotional truth* if not the actual truth. That is good advice in general regarding using your personal experience in all types of creative writing.

Throughout, depend on your growing confidence with the tools of poetry. Use metaphor deliberately; pay attention to your line endings. Let the imagery tell the story, line by line. In the end, reread Kooser's final lines. Let them inspire you to blend the real with the surreal, the common experience with the surreal one.

ALTERNATE MODEL POEM

Out, Out

by Robert Frost

The buzz-saw snarled and rattled in the yard
And made dust and dropped stove-length sticks of wood,
Sweet-scented stuff when the breeze drew across it.
And from there those that lifted eyes could count
Five mountain ranges one behind the other
Under the sunset far into Vermont.
And the saw snarled and rattled, snarled and rattled,
As it ran light, or had to bear a load.
And nothing happened: day was all but done.
Call it a day, I wish they might have said
To please the boy by giving him the half hour
That a boy counts so much when saved from work.
His sister stood beside them in her apron
To tell them "Supper." At the word, the saw,
As if to prove saws knew what supper meant,
Leaped out at the boy's hand, or seemed to leap—
He must have given the hand. However it was,
Neither refused the meeting. But the hand!
The boy's first outcry was a rueful laugh,
As he swung toward them holding up the hand
Half in appeal, but half as if to keep
The life from spilling. Then the boy saw all—
Since he was old enough to know, big boy
Doing a man's work, though a child at heart—
He saw all spoiled. "Don't let him cut my hand off—
The doctor, when he comes. Don't let him, sister!"
So. But the hand was gone already.
The doctor put him in the dark of ether.
He lay and puffed his lips out with his breath.
And then—the watcher at his pulse took fright.
No one believed. They listened at his heart.
Little—less—nothing!—and that ended it.
No more to build on there. And they, since they
Were not the one dead, turned to their affairs.

THE EXPLICATION

Except for the ominous title that alludes to *Macbeth,* this narrative poem begins simply enough with the snarl and rattle of a buzz saw that produced "sweet-scented" sawdust "when the breeze drew across it." Note how the poet sets the poem's situation in near time—the work yard itself—and the locality in general, a place from which the speaker and audience might see "far into Vermont" and five ranges of mountains.

It is the end of the day, and one worker, a "big boy / doing a man's work" is getting ready to leave with his sister who "stood beside them in her apron" letting them all know it is suppertime, time to quit work and go home. As soon as she says this word, a dramatic and terrible event occurs: The boy, whose attention perhaps had been turned away from his task for just a moment toward his sister, loses his hand to the buzz saw in an instant, a horrible instant in which even the boy, shocked and bloodied, "saw all spoiled."

When the doctor arrives, the boy pleads with his sister not to let the doctor cut off his injured hand. "He saw all spoiled," the speaker tells us. The line seems to imply the boy knows his life is ruined, it's all over, yet about the arriving doctor he calls out, "Don't let him cut my hand off!" (Note Frost words it, "The doctor, when he comes . . . ," implying no rush of medical care and using understatement—also called litotes—for effect in the laconic manner of New Englanders.)

The poem's situation has been established; the dramatic climax of the poem occurred. Here in a line that embodies Frost's genius is a use of caesura and spare speech most illustrative for student poets: "So. But the hand was gone already." One word and a period, "So." This is a bold use of caesura. It emphasizes the bizarre and horrible with its very brevity and understatement. Its lack of emotion juxtaposed with the bloody, deadly accident that has just happened emphasizes the horror. Understatement is a powerful tool.

The final third of the poem seems anticlimactic and is as laconic and brief in its delivery of theme: "No more to build on there. And they, since they / Were not the one dead, turned to their affairs." The speaker is blunt. No emotion. No tears on the page. This withdrawal of emotion, this tight control of imagery and line-by-line pragmatism of imagery and events conveys meaning:

These are New Englanders, tough as nails; they are used to death and know how to be survivors, so much so that their lack of reaction seems truly as bizarre as the accident itself; true, anyone's life can be cut short, cut off, in an instant. That's the simple fact.

Frost uses brevity and emotional control to narrate this poem, though he does not always use this technique. Frost seems to suggest with such choices in language and craft tools that life is hard, that survival is a matter of luck, that a hard reality demands a cool head and heart.

ALTERNATE MODEL EXERCISE

Both of these masterful poems are fine examples of uses of narrative in poetry. Using the Frost poem as a model, think of a story that you have heard about someone in town or perhaps in your family. It should be one specific event that occurred at a specific moment and time; brainstorm the concrete details. Go back and delete any common detail; delete any redundant details or word choices.

Now think about your poem as in three parts: The first part sets the poem in time and place. Do so as Frost's poem does it: Begin with the zoom-lens perspective of the precise moment (here as Frost does you might leap *in medias res*, right into the moment of action with no introduction of facts of events). Add an audio image and another sensory one (as Frost uses sound and smell). Step back in your perspective and set down a second image, a wide-angle view. Perhaps it's the cityscape, or landscape; perhaps you choose to use a proper noun here, which might be effective.

In the second part of your poem, the event happens. Take the leap right into the action. Use no adverbs to announce how or when. Offer a line or two of dialogue here. Perhaps the character of focus in your poem declares something, yells something, begs for something. Whatever. Make it surprising. Make sure it is emotionally honest.

Finally, make your turn to the end lines, where you sum up the reaction of those standing by, the observers, the witnesses. How do they react? Do not tell us; show us. Leave us with an image. Show what you have learned from Frost about the deft use of understatement to convey tone and meaning. Title your poem something that alludes to a Shakespearean character or play that adds foreshadowing to the poem's action and theme.

SAMPLE STUDENT POEMS

The Choice

by Ethan Marcus Goode

As the sun drifts nearer the horizon
I stride outside to see her, a dead rat, still cold from the freezer,
clutched in my hand. The sharp clacking of a yellow beak
sounds as I enter her house, place the rat on her food board,
turn to greet her, the barred owl sitting on the highest perch.
Her talons, black as obsidian, peek out from beneath—
Her feathers, speckled like snow on bark, encircle—
Her eyes, deep as a forest pool, stare out of a beautiful predator.
Those eyes once stared, overlarge, out of a tiny fluff ball with stubby wings
who made a makeshift nest from a sideways flowerpot,
who perched on my head and sent a slimy something down my cheek,
who grew into a regal creature sitting on my gloved fist like a queen on her throne,
who lives every day in the same four walls eating the same cold rats.
"That bird is a prisoner in that house," my mother once said to me.
Stroking her soft plumage, I peer into the gathering dark and see her
flying through a twilight forest into a moonlit night,
swooping with a hunter's silence upon an unwary rabbit,
sitting in a nest with four fluffy owlets squabbling for her attentions,
lying on the hard asphalt, a broken mass of bloody feathers.
An icy cold grips my chest as I look back into her eyes.
I know what I will do.

Last Haircut

by Natalie Lyons

It was a Tuesday, and not unusual
at all for her to cut his hair
as he sat on a kitchen chair, an old towel
draped around his broad, tanned shoulders.

His hair was silky blonde, not yet
turned mousy brown from age.
He liked to wear it long but responsibility

required the cut. We had all expected
to see him bald someday, the way blonde men go.

Under the ceiling fan light she fingered
wet hair nonchalantly, straightening and snipping,
pushing his ears forward with her thumbs,
quickly brushing the hairs caught in his eyelashes,
palming his crown, and gently pushing his head
forward to straighten the back.

She didn't know enough to be nervous, but still
she dropped the comb a lot.
If she had only known this was to be the last
time she would touch him alive

she would have caressed each lock, snipped gently
and slowly, savoring the moment. Carefully,
she would have touched his face, memorizing
the angles and feel of it, smoothing them into her
mind, as she brushed his eyebrows carefully
with the tender tips of her fingers.

Torn Shoelace

by Ashley LaRose

for all the lost children

There was an untied shoe floating down
a muddy river, Thursday. Lost there, it remained
caught on a branch, its muscles fought the current,
detached from its owner. His canvas soul hums
a muffled scent as if it were a tune from a record
player. The determined dog stops four miles down.
He lifts his ear, stares just for a moment
but the needle was too dull, the sweet music, distorted.
The shoe calls to its owner: face down across the bank,
fragments of defeat remain clutched in her hand.
A restless search party retraces its steps,
time ticking hard against their will.

To understand would be too somber. They are afraid.
They work. The moon provides light, the stars warmth.
The shoe belonged to a soul, the soul to a body.
She had given up the fight, her chest now hollow.

Sedated by fear, the shoe tries to whisper "double knots"
but she did not hear. The divers find the lost shoe on a Friday,
the orange Chuck Taylor held by a Smokey the Bear shoelace.
A sparrow shyly brushes the girl. Her nostrils flay
open filling her lungs with a tank of relief.
Someone is waiting for her. Her heart beats
like hummingbird wings. Her body feels her eyes smile.
She forgets the word for a moment . . . happiness. The shoe goes limp.
Dogs bark. The search party gathers and departs.
Candles flicker, fragrant smoke fills her room.
They find her on Saturday. Her body—in a silk bed,
two creamsicle high tops at her feet; her soul now safely home.

Overdone and Over and Done

by Chelsea Stulen

I.

It wasn't the bricks of concrete walls
    keeping me safe from the outside world,
    but the taste of freedom lingered.
    Looking out the window, I would ask
    again, each of them would say "Not today."
    Always followed what I was told;
    it still wasn't enough
    to taste the outside.
    The blood, the skin, the immunity,
    was not good enough
    for me. All I would get
    in return were more
    pills, tranquilizers and stares.

II.
Times always seems to remedy
everything, not just pain.
The blood, the skin, the immunity,
is not the best, but is good enough for me.
Looking out the window, I would ask
again, each of them would say "Yes"
what I always wanted to hear.
I return, always thinking
of the old prison.
He's not here, and neither is she.
The feeling of imprisonment
has evaporated with them.
Time took those thoughts.
Now, I can go.

NOTE

REFERENCE

Kooser, Ted. *The Poetry Home Repair Manual: Practical Advice for Beginning Poets.* Lincoln: University of Nebraska Press, 2005.

Chapter Eight

Communicating Emotional Truths and Avoiding Melodrama

We want some of that human heat. Each of us who writes must find a balance between restraint and expressions of feeling.

—Ted Kooser, from *The Poetry Home Repair Manual*
(Kooser 2005, 57)

Perhaps one way to distinguish simple verse from real art is the line drawn firmly in the sand that disallows sentimentality. Sentiment, yes; sentimentality, never. Sometimes poets-in-learning tend toward the melodramatic, thinking that to express themselves they need to offer wild, uncontrolled emotions.

Frequently, the problem with such poems is that they are out of control. It may seem counterintuitive, but powerful emotion in poetry is better handled deftly, deliberately, and in controlled fashion. Also, poems of that type sometimes tell readers how to feel and tell readers how the speaker feels, rather than relying on strong images to convey situation, action, and meaning.

Melodrama, like soap operas on television, dumbs down the human experience; too much crying and yelling. Too much hysteria and exclamation! (like this). Characters tell each other things that could be implied through better writing or more artful acting. Soap operas embrace sentimentality and play it to the hilt. Get out the violins! Soap opera emotion and melodrama lead to sentimentality, a tough word to define. It means an excess of uncontrolled emotion. It is a kind of overplaying the scene. Even fans of soap operas must laugh when this happens.

So what does that have to do with poetry? Plenty. Art is a tricky mistress. She must be coddled and adored; she needs kid gloves and champagne, coaxing and understated wardrobes. The poem is art; that's the goal. Better to err on the side of understatement.

Here's what we tell our students in workshop: When you write, expect readers, your audience, to *get it*. Expect the audience to be well and widely read, to have the sensibility to get your drift and make leaps with you in a poem. When poets explain everything, they are talking down to readers; they are assuming readers won't get it.

Too much telling and overtelling, too many adverbs and adjectives equal the dumbing down of writing. It is rather insulting to the audience as well. Students should know this: Assume the audience writes poetry well and knows as much about poetry or more than they do. That is the audience.

If writers learn to do that, it will restrain their desire *to explain and repeat*. It will allow a freedom of expression that is a venue for true voices to come through. Better to whisper and allow readers to lean in.

Part of this tricky business is to be aware of sentimentality and its better-dressed cousin, honest sentiment. Sentimentality wears too much makeup, is too blond, too loud, and just too much; sentiment walks into a room and everyone says, ah, she is a well-dressed and impeccable lady.

Poet Laureate Ted Kooser speaks at length about avoiding sentimentality in his fine book *The Poetry Home Repair Manual.* In brief, Kooser suggests it is best "to skate along the edge of sentimentality without careening off the edge" (57). He also terms sentimentality "gushiness (58)."

Students will know this kind of behavior. It's Aunt Agnes who gushes about all her child's achievements while everybody in the family rolls their eyes; it's the superfan who can't stop telling the quarterback how great he is. It's too many words and too little control. Get it? Greeting cards, poems written just to share with lovers and those who love us, can enjoy sentimentality all they want.

But poets who wish to create art and not kitsch, art and not verse, must strive to stay safely away from the maudlin and the sentimental. That does not mean that strong poems can't express deep, complex, and profound emotion. Of course they can, and they do. They do it with an ear for sophisticated control of emotional expression.

Part of it has to do with showing through imagery rather than telling the reader or editorializing for the reader how the speaker feels. Let's reinforce that point: *Poets should not editorialize.* In fact, if they do that, it really is not art; it really is not poetry. Neither, we might add, should poetry be didactic or instructive to readers. That is, they should not tell readers how the character in the poem feels nor tell the reader how to feel. Instead, they would do better to show emotion through strong and unique imagery.

Remember, poets should be striving for control over their emotions and should let the imagery speak. In the model poem, readers will see how poems of great emotional depth show restraint.

TERMS USED IN THIS CHAPTER

Dichotomy: The ironic situation wherein two polar opposite truths or things exist at the same time.

Literal versus Figurative: Literal interpretation means according to concrete and unarguable facts; figurative interpretation, on the other hand, demands a creative drawing of inference from facts and imagery. Figurative is a higher critical thinking skill, but it must be based on a concrete foundation.

Pacing: Part of the prosody of poetry wherein the poet's ear uses a certain kind of musical sense of meter or rhythm to pace the narration of the poem and to control the reader's intake of information. It involves punctuation and phrasing. Caesura and enjambment are thus integral elements of pacing, tools for the craft of poetry.

Sentimentalism/Sentimentality: Whereas sentimentality is a type of too much expression of one emotion to the point of excess or to a point of maudlin, sentiment is the controlled and restrained conveyance of emotion in a strong poem. Ted Kooser advises poets never to trip over the edge of sentiment into sentimentality, but he admits he often walks a fine line between the two. In any case, it is the best advice to poets. The point is to handle emotion deftly, to offer nuance, and to allow imagery to tell the "story" of any poem without editorial emotions. Avoid the crying, we tell our students; no crying in poetry, we remind our story. Let the readers cry; keep the crying out of the poetry.

Tension/Ambivalence: A necessary emotional ingredient for most well-crafted poems. Tension is the conflict between reality and desire and/or between contrasting emotions and desires in a given work of art. Such ambivalence of emotion heightens emotion and creates a stronger poem.

THE MODEL POEM

Osteosarcoma: A Love Poem
for Easton, Zooey, and Nacho

by Yvonne Zipter

Cancer loves the long bone,
the femur and the fibula,
the humerus and ulna,
the greyhound's sleek physique,
a calumet, ribboned with fur
and eddies of dust churned to a smoke,
the sweet slenderness of that languorous
lick of calcium, like an ivory flute or a stalk
of Spiegelau stemware, its bowl
bruised, for an eye blink, with burgundy,
a reed, a wand, the violin's bow—
loves the generous line of your lanky limbs,
the distance between points A and D,
epic as Western Avenue, which never seems to end
but then of course it does, emptying
its miles into the Cal-Sag Channel
that river of waste and sorrow.
I've begun a scrapbook:
here the limp that started it all, here
your scream when the shoulder bone broke,
here that walk to the water dish,
your leg trailing like a length
of black bunting. And here the words I whispered
when your ears lay like spent milkweed pods
on that beautiful silky head:
Run, Run, my boy-o,
in that madcap zigzag,
unzipping the air.

THE EXPLICATION

When writing about a loss, it is so difficult not to fall into sentimental-ism, losing the poem's beautiful resilience. In her poem "Osteosarcoma: A Love Poem," Yvonne Zipter writes about losing her dog to a particular bone cancer. The poem is dramatic and poignant; it is not melodramatic or maudlin.

Notice how Zipter begins the poem with three lines that draw attention to bones: "long," sleek bones of the greyhound, "the femur and fibula, / the humerus and ulna. . . ." Readers instinctively know these medical terms represent the longer bones in the body. The medical terms call at-tention to serious illness, in this case, a fatal cancer. The speaker says, "the greyhound's sleek physique." This description follows the first word in the poem: "Cancer," so that the reader knows without question that this dog has agonizing bone cancer.

Next the speaker begins to layer object upon object in order to illustrate the beauty of the bones. First the poem compares the bones to a calumet, a long, thin Native American pipe adorned with feathers. The line goes on to say, "ribboned with fur / and eddies of dust churned to a smoke. . . ." Clearly, the speaker intends the reader to connect the death of her loving pet to ritual, a direct way to preserve the sanctity of her feelings, not to mention the pipe has a certain grace itself.

Zipter layers the imagery throughout. She writes "the sweet slenderness of that languorous / lick of calcium," referring directly to the dog's bones. The reader sees the sweetness, the "slenderness," and might translate this into a dreamy, almost lazy "lick of calcium" connected to an "ivory flute" in the same line. The poet seems to juxtapose the beauty of the bones when healthy with the horror of the fatal bone cancer.

The enjambed line flows into the "lick of calcium" quickly, then has a slight break with a comma before the "ivory flute." There is a distinct calmness and beauty when one aligns sweet, slender, languorous, and ivory in the same image, plus the bones are compared to a musical flute, which seems to add a rather mystical quality to the image.

Zipter describes the long bone as "a stalk / of Spiegelau stemware, its bowl / bruised, for an eye blink, with burgundy," an apt and powerful metaphor.

The poem spills down the page in lines with deep emotion yet without sentimentality. From the first word, "cancer," no period stops readers until line 17. That is enjambment used effectively. The form fits the poem's meaning; it's as if cancer's journey is fast and merciless, just as the reader zips through the poem from top to bottom.

The speaker has "begun a scrapbook." She lists three powerful images of the cancer's progression, which end with caesura in the fifth line. Zipter is careful to relate each painful memory as a matter of fact: "here the limp that started it all, here / your scream when the shoulder bone broke, / here that walk to the water dish, / your leg trailing like a length /of black bunting." Each image carries its own special memory of loss.

The last section of the poem begins in the middle of a line: "And here the words I whispered /when your ears lay like spent milkweed pods / on that beautiful head: *Run, Run, my boy-o / in that madcap zigzag, / unzipping the air.*" It's a heartbreaking couple of lines, a haunting phrasing. Zipter uses alliteration in the last two lines, which makes the lines musical, yet quite real. The sound of the *z* pulls those two lines together, and the reader can almost hear the speaker whispering into the dog's ear. Notice first there are two enjambed lines, then a colon, then two with commas, and the poem ends with an end-stopped line.

Think of the difference it would have made if the poem had ended with ellipses instead of being end-stopped. Zipter's punctuation is exquisite here. First the lines move quickly, followed by a long pause with the colon, two slight pauses with commas, and finally a full stop at the end.

This poem is truly a love poem that deals with the relationship of loving and losing, two parts of the same, as C. S. Lewis says. It contains both the love and the loss of the dog. In a sense, the poem memorializes the dog through images and photographs, each one giving the reader more access to the nature and beauty of a relationship between the owner and her pet.

The true power of this poem lies in the poet's artful ability to offer fresh, startling imagery and to deal with death and grief with great control. Quite a feat in a remarkable poem.

EXERCISES FOR STUDENTS

Quick Exercise 1. Practice in Emotional Distancing (15 minutes)

In your mind's eye, capture a time when you or someone you know experienced a traumatic or difficult experience. Perhaps it was the illness and death of a person or a beloved pet. Do not write about anything you are uncomfortable sharing with your group or anything that has a whiff of revenge or mean-spiritedness from your own perspective. You might also write about a moment, a time when something difficult happened to you. One example might be to write about a moment from high school, middle school, or elementary school that you remember vividly. See Peggy Aiello's award-winning student poem at the end of the chapter called "Ninth Grade," for example. Your job is to remember something tough and to put it down on the page in images, not feelings. *Images not feelings.* List the images one by one. Try to put them down on the page as an artist would paint the varied images.

Quick Exercise 2. Editing out Adverbs, Judgmental Words, or Telling Readers How to Feel (15 to 20 minutes)

Go back over your images line by line, editing out all adverbs, judgmental words, or any language that explains too much or tries to tell readers how they should feel about the experience you are describing. Leave just the facts listed in the imagery.

Now reread the imagery to see how effective each line is in capturing the important and unique details. Did you create one good metaphor such as Zipter does with equating the long bone to Spiegelau crystal? A strong simile instead? Why one or the other? Make a deliberate choice. Finally, add a final line now that somehow sums up the experience without telling readers how to feel or how *you* feel.

THE MODEL EXERCISE

Use the quick exercises 1 and 2 if you completed them.

Write a poem about an incident you vividly remember from your childhood. It might or might not be a personally painful or emotionally fraught one. It could just be a significant moment from your youth. If you did not use quick exercise 1 as an initial prompt, read it now for an idea about an incident from school that would work for this poem.

Hold on now: This assignment is a tough one. It calls on courage of reflection; it calls up painful memories and images. But this exercise can lead you to a fine poem. So here it is: Write a poem about something that happened *to you* or *someone you know* in your childhood years. It could be a car accident, an abusive parent, a drunken uncle, whatever; we all have painful memories from our own experience or from others' lives. Rilke says if we only used our childhoods, we would have enough material to write about for a lifetime.

Remember: This does not have to be about you. Don't try to tackle any emotional memories too difficult to put down on the page.

Use this poem as your model, following the stanzas, line endings, and use of elements in it as your guide. Use your tools of line endings, enjambment, and caesura to create tension from line to line and control the pace. Make the reader hold her breath, waiting for the next line. Decide on how to handle the stanzas: What would best serve the poem? One longer stanza? Many short stanzas? Be deliberate about it.

Most importantly in this exercise, your goal is to retain control of the speaker. Create one that can tell the emotional truth of a difficult or tragic event without expressing melodramatic emotion; create a speaker who is controlled and who can lay the lines down with dignity and purpose. Choose your speaker's point of view thoughtfully—is it first person? Is it a second-person speaker? Which better serves the poem? Is your speaker an observer or a victim? If this experience happened to you, try shifting into the third person instead. That technique offers you personally some emotional control from the experience and more control over your speaker. Write about yourself as "she," as "her," as that girl or woman, or as "he," "him," and that boy or man.

Try to avoid shedding tears of any kind in the poem; avoid telling the reader how you or someone else felt. You have learned that to say a tear rolled down someone's cheek is a banal observation. Your job as a poet is to witness the unusual, to lay down the words in a unique and fresh way that shares the emotional truth if not the actual or realistic truth.

Keep in mind at every turn and every word choice not to slip into the mire of sentimentality. Err if you must on the side of understatement. This is a test of your control as a poet. Sentiment, powerful sentiment—yes! Sentimentality, never. Melodrama, no.

Find the imagistic keys that show the reader what you intend. Edit and pare until no sentimentality is expressed. Play Frost. Be blunt. Understate your drama. And believe this: The more you hold back, the more powerful the effect, dramatically.

SAMPLE STUDENT POEMS

Ninth Grade

by Peggy Aiello

Dressed in another's cast-offs,
aware of how they drape
her boyish frame,
no other girl on earth could be this dreary.
She steps around the corner and down the hall.
Jejune boys huddled at the bend in the hallway—
watching over pedestrian students.
She clings to the lockers
wishing they could swallow her in.
The passage too narrow to slip by,
no place to go to avoid their whispers
and foolhardy laughter. What callous observation
would those tinsel teeth reveal today?
Raising her chin and passing the lair
there are no comments betrayed
this day: she bedamns them
for making
her feel
so
unlovely.

Bipolar: A Lifelong Hurricane

by Allison Weatherly

Your disease doesn't have a season.
It is year round. There's no warning.
No one to rate how bad it will be next.
I can't enjoy the calm. The dimmer
the sun shines, the flatter the wren
sings and the heavier the air breathes;
I wait for your impact. The longer
it lasts, I know, the bigger the storm
will be. After you're done ripping
the trees off of their roots, I'm left alone
again, to pick up after you. When I finally
put my life back together, the clouds scatter,
the sun starts to shine, and I just wait
here bracing myself for the next storm surge
while a wren taunts me with its music.

Over

by Nicole Torino

Sunday morning—family prim and proper.
Car flows along the black sea;
three girls sing merrily in ignorant bliss.

My father's eyes distant yet alert.
He never looks to the passenger side;
she sighs, sending aggravated vibes.

A halt in the fellowship, "Intensive Care"
sounds like some rigorous therapy.
Smiles, embraces all around,

we all venture to our respectful places.
I look before I depart—
their emotions are not covered easily.

At twelve I can see someone is unraveling,
I pretend not to notice,
but by noon, it's already over.

Lost Voice

by Natalie Lyons

My friend was fat;
but that didn't stop
Dad from his disgusting game; you touch
me here, let me touch
you there. She tried to reach
me later, but shame
caused me to ignore the voice
only the innocent
lose.

NOTE

Credit: Yvonne Zipter, "Osteosarcoma: A Love Poem." Reprinted by permission of Yvonne Zipter.

REFERENCE

Kooser, Ted. *The Poetry Home Repair Manual: Practical Advice for Beginning Poets*. Lincoln: University of Nebraska Press, 2005.

Chapter Nine

Writing in Other Voices

"By trying other people on for size, you can transcend every one of your physical/temporal limitations. You can change your sex, you can live in the past or future. . . . You can climb a mountain."

—Lola Haskins, from *Not Feathers Yet: A Beginner's Guide to the Poetic Life* (Haskins 2007, 119)

Sometimes a poet chooses to write a poem in another person's voice. This is an interesting craft technique. One can choose to write in the voice of some imagined character or in the voice of an ancestor, someone who did, indeed, live in the world at some time. It might be the voice of an imagined character.

Writing in another person's voice requires a certain level of imagination, trying to climb into another person's mind and "voice" their thoughts on the page. This is a wonderful technique for beginning poets, as it gives writers both an idea and a reference point. For example, in the book titled *Markers*, Suzanne Keyworth writes a poem in the voice of her stepfather during Christmastime.

Keyworth uses personal history to attempt to speak in his voice from his point of view. No one can truly know someone else's point of view, but it is an interesting exercise to try to write a poem in this way. The poem seems to be generated from Keyworth's background and experience; however, this does not mean the poem is absolutely accurate.

This kind of writing shows students the difference between poet and speaker; it shows students the speaker is always an artificial thing, created for a particular purpose.

Anyone can write a poem using another person's voice. It is a technique used by many famous poets and offers an outlet to someone who doesn't want to expose certain material about himself or herself. Sometimes this kind of poem takes the form of dramatic monologue, particularly when the poem is a long, narrative style like Browning's "My Last Duchess."

However, poets can also assume the guise of someone else's voice in a lyric poem. The distinction between the two is minimal. Why not use a strategy available to all poets for writing a poem about something sensitive in life without having to expose anything considered personal to the writer? Voice is a critical technique that all poets need to practice, and creating voice and character are important tools of the craft.

TERMS USED IN THIS CHAPTER

Dramatic Monologue: A dramatic monologue is a type of poem in which the poet assumes the voice of another person in order to narrate a story or "tell" about a specific event. The poet assumes the persona of the other person in action, movement, speech, and attitude. It is the poetic form most akin to drama and acting, and a type of poem that inherently shows without telling some kind of personal secret truth.

Lyric: Lyric is a brief poem about emotions; the term comes from ancient bards who composed and sang ballads. Lyric today refers to any short poem of emotion.

Voice: Voice involves the spoken words on the page in a poem that resemble and echo the natural speaker's voice. In this chapter, voice refers to assuming another person's persona and all its dimensions of being (sound, action, verbiage, pacing, tone).

THE MODEL POEM

Stepfather Harold Albert Dickson
March 23, 1912–November 28, 1978

by Suzanne Keyworth

Afraid of fire,
I stood the evergreen

in a five gallon pail,
filled it to the brim.
I plugged in the lights,
checked each bulb, ran my fingers
along the wires, wound thin, black tape
over the bare spots, joined the strings,
my favorite the bubble
lights brought down from the North.
Like tiny candles without flames,
like the breath of small children behind glass,
they glistened on the tips of twigs, and the children were
star gazers, watching each ornament
emerge like a crystal globe in my hand.
Spirals of glass, ringlets of gold,
the tree grew large, the whole season's
promise at its feet, and sometimes
if the children were careful, if they held the strands
just so, I let them cover the lower branches
in tinsel, one thread at a time,
one small hand giving way
to another, silver against green,
their hearts stood in line, their fingers
touched and trembled beneath my stare.
It was beautiful really.
It was perfectly arranged.
Mother on the couch.
The children like small lamps.
The sound of silver bells.

THE EXPLICATION

Poets create speakers to use as the voice of their poems. Their choices in voice change from poem to poem, according to the content, focus, and theme. In some poems, long, dramatic ones, this technique can be called dramatic monologue (see the Browning poem later on in the chapter). In shorter lyric poems, it is just a decision regarding point of view.

Keyworth's poem is titled in the name of her stepfather, Harold Albert Dickson. It is his voice who speaks, his memory that tells the story. In so doing, the poet herself steps away from the situation and views the world from the perspective of someone else entirely. This can be an effective and useful technique.

The poet intends for the reader to immediately recognize that the speaker in this poem is her imagined stepfather performing the task of bringing in the Christmas tree and adorning it with bulbs and lights. She also intends for the reader to assume she is one of the "small lamps" seated on the floor at the foot of the decorated tree. Imagining a given speaker for a poem is a craft tool that allows the poet a sense of distance from the content of the poem.

After all, what this speaker will do and say is left entirely up to the poet's imagination. All poems are imagined, but not all poems present a particular speaker the reader can recognize. The stepfather tells the story of this event through his memory, a memory completely imagined by Keyworth.

The poem begins with a short line, just three words: "Afraid of fire. . . ." The line break and comma offer a moment before the reader goes on to listen to the speaker say: "I stood the evergreen. . . ." At this point, the reader might be imagining Christmas as the speaker stands an evergreen "in a five gallon pail. . . ." The reader now recognizes a Christmas tree and for some reason, the stepfather, out of his fear of fire, feels the need to place the tree in a five-gallon pail.

In the subsequent line, the stepfather fills this five-gallon pail "to the brim," surely an indication that he fears fire. The reader may wonder if some past incident haunts his mind and if he personally witnessed a Christmas-tree fire at his own home. Notice how the writer layers the images so that the reader gets one short view after another until the whole picture becomes visible.

By the end of line 4, readers can see the whole image. In some ways this craft technique hurries the pace of the poem by using short, clipped sentences rather than the longer, more languid line. This technique moves the reader quickly down through the lines even though each line contains a brief, subtle break with each line. Even so, the lines are so short that the pace quickens.

The stepfather continues, "I plugged in the lights / checked each bulb, ran my fingers / along the wires, wound thin, black tape / over the bare spots, joined the strings, / my favorite the bubble / lights brought down from the North." Notice again how the poet uses concrete details and shorter lines to communicate this sorting through lights and making them *safe* to place on the tree.

We have lights, fingers, tape, strings, bubble, and North. These are interesting line breaks that serve to increase the momentum of the poem by enjambing the lines, so that the reader moves quickly on to the next.

Sometimes in a poem, pacing becomes very important. In this case, the reader is in the mind of the stepfather as he moves very quickly from one thought to another. The writer creates a faster-paced poem because it more nearly captures the voice of a character. People speak at a faster pace than one can often read, so the writer picks up the pace of the written word here.

Now some of the more dramatic images begin. "Like tiny candles without flames, / like the breath of small children behind glass, / they glistened on the tips of twigs, and the children were / star gazers, watching each ornament / emerge like a crystal globe in my hand." The voice in the poem, the thoughts of the speaker, drift back to the sight of those bubble lights and what they looked like on the trees.

Now the writer chooses to lengthen a line, to slow down the pace of the poem for a moment so that the reader takes time to see the bubble lights and those children, those "star gazers," as they watch the stepfather's every move. The poet tries to help the reader visualize these bubble lights, as if they are "tiny candles with flames," and "the breath of small children behind glass."

If readers have ever seen the lights they used to call "bubble lights," they will recognize those candle-shaped bulbs made of glass, which heat up and have bubbles going up through the liquid color. They are lovely on a Christmas tree, and apparently the stepfather remembers them from when he was a child. Therefore, he purchases them for his own children to see.

Notice how the line that ends with the odd word "were" stretches out on the page and slows the pace of the poem, draws out the pace by its length, and then suddenly on the next line there are "star gazers," the image of the children watching the stepfather at work on the Christmas tree. The magic begins here. The poem's pace slows.

The poet wants the reader to take note of these young "star gazers," so rather than put them on the same line with "the children were," she lets the reader read through the longer line, slows the pacing, and presents them first on the next line. These "star gazers" are "watching each ornament / emerge like a crystal globe in my hand," the stepfather says.

And the poem pauses with the end-stopped line. The stepfather describes "Spirals of glass, ringlets of gold / the tree grew large, the whole season's / promise at its feet. . . ." The images here of ornaments like crystal globes and spirals of glass or ringlets of gold make the poem come to life with the festive feel of Christmas and the awe children experience when dressing the Christmas tree.

It seems obvious the stepfather loves Christmas and willingly spends his time donning the tree for the children to enjoy. Now, however, there's a trace of something new, something a bit darker. The stepfather wants the tree to be exactly right, and as a result only sometimes does he let the children help: " . . . and sometimes / if the children were careful, if they held the strands / just so, I let them cover the lower branches / in tinsel, one thread at a time, / one small hand giving way / to another, silver against green, / their hearts stood in line, their fingers / touched and trembled beneath my stare."

This word picture suggests that he is a perfectionist when it comes to Christmas trees (and the implication is, in every aspect of life as well), thus he fears the children might not do a perfect job. He hovers over them to the point that it makes them scared they might place the tinsel not *just so* as required by the stepfather.

Here is the emotional heart of the poem. Readers must pay attention. So what? How does this kind of hypervigilance affect children and their sense of self? Would they grow up feeling confident and sure? Or might they grow up lacking in self-confidence and worrying too much that whatever they do is not perfect, not perfect enough for the stepparent's approval?

This isn't just guessing on the part of good readers. There's evidence: The children want desperately to please and participate; they are willing to endure the stepfather's judgmental gaze. But they would not be trembling if his stare was kindly. The innocence of the children is so great, their "hearts stood in line." Imagine these young children under the glare of their stepfather's eyes. Imagine how they are willing to withstand that glare if only to place a few strands of tinsel on the tree.

Now the poet changes the pace of the poem entirely, using four short sentences with end-stopped lines. This slows the poem down substantially and accentuates each sentence. The stepfather says first, "It was beautiful really." Does he refer to the Christmas tree itself or the action of the young children at the foot of the tree? Is the beauty he sees something he doesn't even realize, as it may involve the activity of the children he glares at? In either case, the stepfather feels all of this fuss over the tree brings out the beauty, and in some way includes the children in the moment.

That is the poem's irony—even amidst the discomfort produced by the perfectionist, judgmental stepparent, the children's joy and courage make it a beautiful moment. The stepfather recognizes this, and seems to nod in approval, even surprised a bit at his own comment, "It was beautiful really." Readers can hear in that a man who tried so hard. In such hard trying sometimes lies too harsh a judgment of oneself and of others, loved ones in particular. The story of this family is told through one event. The speaker does not seem to realize how much of himself he gives away.

Next the stepfather says: "It was perfectly arranged." Ah, so perhaps even though the children placed tinsel on the bottom of the tree, they managed to please him in spite of his glare. Pleased with their work and with his own, perhaps together they have made the tree good enough for a perfectionist. Notice how the end-stopped line causes the reader to pause after each sentence and consider these sentences for a longer period of time, much longer than if the lines were enjambed. These harshly end-stopped lines seem to lend fear, apprehension, a nervous quality to the poem, as if such perfection is impossible and will not last. It is a tremulous perfection. It imprints on these children.

"Mother on the couch. / The children like small lamps." Both of these lines are end-stopped. The stepfather looks around the room during this Christmas season and recognizes that his wife sits on the couch, the children sit on the floor "like small lamps," and everything becomes "perfectly arranged." This is both bad and good, this perfect arrangement of the tree, the lights, the tinsel, their lives.

The speaker takes in the whole picture, which includes the tree, and his wife, and his children as well. Everything seems to be the perfect picture of Christmas to him. In spite of his perfectionist nature, the room has managed somehow to complete his picture of Christmas and be "perfect" at the same time.

Writing in another's voice can be challenging and rewarding. It can offer the poet new perspective on old memories and situations. It can bring people to life by imagining how they speak and what they say. It can, if done well, offer insights into the human heart and the human family of experience, as it does in this poem.

EXERCISES FOR STUDENTS

Quick Exercise 1. Turning a Holiday into a Poem (15 minutes)

Think back. Travel down that long stretch of life's memories. Brainstorm a list of holidays you remember in detail. The last Christmas grandma was alive—how your family celebrated at her house, how she prepared at length for the special day and made her fabulous corn pudding, for example.

Or maybe how every Easter Sunday your mother would buy you a new purse or a new dress. Maybe it was that Fourth of July when Uncle Sherman got drunk and said awful things to his wife in front of the family. Take a look at your list. Which one might you write about in a way that would show underlying meaning as Keyworth does in her poem about living with a stepparent?

Which one might allow you to write from a point of view quite different from your own—your stepmother's? Your grandfather's? Spend some time just thinking. Make a decision. Generate some lines of imagery about that holiday.

Quick Exercise 2: Writing in Another's Voice (20 minutes)

Think about the person whose voice you intend to use to speak the poem. What did that person sound like? What kinds of words did he or she use? Was there a familiar phrasing? A common adage often repeated? What level of diction? What tone and attitude? Now jot these things down to get you started. Say a line in the speaker's voice. Try it on. Write another line in the speaker's voice. Come up with five or six things you can hear that person saying. Try to capture the essence of their personality in your words. Good. Next you will marry the images with the speaker's voice.

THE MODEL EXERCISE

Write a poem from someone else's perspective and with someone else's voice. Assume the voice of somebody else, someone you knew well and listened to regularly. Use the language they used. Select the voice (attitude, tone, diction, physical attributes) of a family member you knew well and loved, revered, feared, or better yet, had ambivalent feelings about.

Show that relative engaged in one particular task, such as the speaker in the model poem putting up a Christmas tree and facilitating its trimming by his children with a judgmental eye. It's important to pick a single physical action that clearly puts the poem in time and space. Start there. If you used quick exercises 1 and 2 as earlier prompts, use what you discovered there to get you started.

Establish your point of view and consider the diction. *Listen in your memory to this person's voice;* recall physical traits, bodily gestures that indicated emotion and intention. What phrases were used frequently? What words and gestures illustrate that person's character and personality? Try brainstorming a list of images. Of course, most important is to choose descriptors and create imagery that shows rather than tells the audience the truth about this person and about your relationship perhaps with this person.

Use that opening line to place your speaker and his action. Use concrete descriptors such as size, color, shape, and the five senses as applicable to create strong imagery. Add yourself or others into the poem. Show yourself and others in descriptive and perhaps metaphoric language. Most importantly, use the craft technique of pacing that Keyworth's poem illustrates so well: Use enjambment, caesura, and punctuation to pause, move, and control your reader from line to line, creating prosody that leads toward meaning.

ALTERNATE MODEL POEM

My Last Duchess

by Robert Browning

That's my last Duchess painted on the wall,
Looking as if she were alive. I call
That piece a wonder, now: Fra Pandolf's hands
Worked busily a day, and there she stands.
Will't please you sit and look at her? I said
"Fra Pandolf" by design, for never read

Strangers like you that pictured countenance,
The depth and passion of its earnest glance,
But to myself they turned (since none puts by
The curtain I have drawn for you, but I)
And seemed as they would ask me, if they durst,
How such a glance came there; so, not the first
Are you to turn and ask thus. Sir, 'twas not
Her husband's presence only, called that spot
Of joy into the Duchess' cheek: perhaps
Fra Pandolf chanced to say "Her mantle laps
Over my lady's wrist too much," or "Paint
Must never hope to reproduce the faint
Half-flush that dies along her throat": such stuff
Was courtesy, she thought, and cause enough
For calling up that spot of joy. She had
A heart—how shall I say?—too soon made glad
Too easily impressed; she liked whate'er
She looked on, and her looks went everywhere.
Sir, 'twas all one! My favour at her breast
The dropping of the daylight in the West,
The bough of cherries some officious fool
Broke in the orchard for her, the white mule
She rode with round the terrace—all and each
Would draw from her alike the approving speech,
Or blush, at least. She thanked men,—good! but thanked
Somehow—I know not how—as if she ranked
My gift of a nine-hundred-years-old name
With anybody's gift. Who'd stoop to blame
This sort of trifling? Even had you skill
In speech—(which I have not)—to make your will
Quite clear to such an one, and say, "Just this
Or that in you disgusts me; here you miss,
Or there exceed the mark"—and if she let
Herself be lessoned so, nor plainly set
Her wits to yours, forsooth, and made excuse,
E'en then would be some stooping; and I choose
Never to stoop. Oh sir, she smiled, no doubt,
Whene'er I passed her; but who passed without

Much the same smile? This grew; I gave commands;
Then all smiles stopped together. There she stands
As if alive. Will't please you rise? We'll meet
The company below, then. I repeat,
The Count your master's known munificence
Is ample warrant that no just pretense
Of mine for dowry will be disallowed;
Though his fair daughter's self, as I avowed
At starting, is my object. Nay, we'll go
Together down, sir. Notice Neptune, though,
Taming a sea-horse, thought a rarity,
Which Claus of Innsbruck cast in bronze for me!

ALTERNATE MODEL EXERCISE

Browning's poem spoken in the voice of the dreadful Duke of Ferrara changes us forever as poets and readers. We might have included it in the chapter on turns or on surprises, as it does both with aplomb. This poem teaches readers to pay attention, to listen for hidden agendas, to never believe the surface story, to not be fooled by manners and charm.

For under the civilized opening lines and guise of the speaker, "That's my last Duchess. . . . Looking as if she were alive," exists both threat and murderer. The threat, if missed by the emissary, may cost the Duke's next young wife her life.

The duke cloaks his murder cleverly and makes a brutal turn in the end as well when he goes from "There she stands / As if alive" to "Notice Neptune . . . Which Claus of Innsbruck cast in bronze for me!" A confession of murder, a threat to murder any other wife who has "—how shall I say?—too soon made glad," and a declaration of utter power: The duke can do as he pleases, for his "nine-hundred-years-old name" grants him permission.

Really, this Browning poem teaches poets so much about the tools of the craft. Most students and readers don't even hear the end rhyme the first few reads through because it is so subtle and Browning's iambic pentameter is so deft. Nobody, nobody, in this century or the past centuries, uses caesura and enjambment with greater effect. Look how Browning, for example, admits the murder and heightens its power with the harsh caesura:

> " . . . This grew; I gave commands
> Then all smiles stopped together. There she stands
> As if alive. Will't please you rise? . . . "

The periods midline smack of doom. The end of the duchess's life is illustrated by those periods. Remember how master poets use punctuation and tools like caesura and enjambment.

But what makes this poem so powerful is Browning's mastery of the dramatic monologue. Browning assumes the voice, persona, cloak, and demeanor of the duke; in so doing, he lets the duke hang himself in his own cleverness.

Note the double irony in the duke's maintaining he has no "skill in speech," all the while deftly maneuvering the emissary to his will coupled with the reader's own recognition that the duke has skill in speech but he admits to murder, has no conscience—a sociopath perhaps—and shows himself to be a monster, not a decent man.

The wit of this kind of entendre is simply stunning. Students can learn from this poem how to write in a voice not their own to tell a story that may or may not be their own. It doesn't matter. What matters is that poets recognize all the elements inherent in character.

This kind of poem demands a bit of playacting and playwriting skill. First, choose a character from history. Read up on this person; know the facts, and weave those facts into your poem. Title your poem in a way that hints at meaning and offers a subtitle that identifies the speaker.

Jot down a list of character traits and other details of the character you wish to assume in the first-person voice. Think of the way such a character phrases, how fast or slowly he or she speaks, how familiar he is, what kinds of language she chooses. Then put on the "clothes" of that individual.

Even better if you can create a character who thinks he or she is clever yet shows to readers he or she is not. This is a poem that must be shared aloud and read by the poet. Do not overdramatize; let the language carry the weight of meaning.

Try to use the Browning end-rhyme pattern; allow it to be a long poem of more than thirty lines.

SAMPLE STUDENT POEMS

Uncle Barry "Buck" Irland

by Drenda Stack

Born 1956 Palmyra, Nebraska

In sixth grade my eyes went black,
for a short time.
I had a chemistry set and big ideas.
Homemade helium in a Pepsi bottle was old news—
aluminum foil balls fizzed like Pop Rocks atop
Crystal Drano and water; jar burned hotter than the welt on my butt
I'd later get from my dad.

Luff left, said his mom was calling him for dinner;
I know he heard that boom,
just kept on a'runnin.

Big idea was to do it in the Palmyra
DRA; arm cocked back,
it materialized,
sparkling shards of shattered illusions.
All I saw for the next four months were clips
of my entire existence—leading up to my date
with darkness.

Great Grandfather

by Tricia Windowmaker

I lifted the axe
and brought it back down again.
Never enough warmth
for all those winter nights.

I wiped the sweat from my brow
and in that moment I heard
the birds chirp, the laughter
of my boy in the background.

I felt the crisp breeze;
the heightened sound of ruffled leaves.
I felt a pain in my left arm
and just like that, I was gone.

NOTE

Credit: Suzanne Keyworth, "Step-father Harold Albert Dickson" appeared in *Markers*, published by Mayapple Press in 2005. Used by permission.

REFERENCE

Haskins, Lola. *Not Feathers Yet: A Beginner's Guide to the Poetic Life*. Omaha, NE: The Backwaters Press, 2007.

Chapter Ten

Sound Devices

The sound is the gold in the ore.

—Robert Frost

Throughout literature, poets use imagery, metaphor, line endings, line break techniques, turns, and epiphanies with finesse and artfulness. The previous chapters have offered examples of these elements of poetic craft through a variety of poems. In this chapter, another integral element of poetic craft will be examined, that of sound devices.

Mary Oliver says in her fine handbook for poets that master poets produce "near-miracles of sound-and-sense" (27–28). Poets choose words for their definitions both literal and abstract and their denotative and connotative meanings, but just as much for their sound value. Or perhaps we could conclude that the connotative, abstract value of any word rests in its sound.

Sound also includes the prosody of the poem. *Prosody* means the way all elements of sound and rhythm and rhyme work together to produce a sort of melody. No doubt readers will not be surprised by this, as many writers see close comparisons between music lyrics and poetry.

There are, nonetheless, serious differences that distinguish the two, and there should be. In lyrics, musicians rely on refrains and verses, usually exact or near rhyme; elements of poetic tools may be used, particularly by gifted songwriters, but lyrics and songs rely on the music itself. What is repetition for good effect in song lyrics may be simply redundant and boring in poems. In contrast, poems rely on nuance, clarity of image, creative analogies, leaps of imagination; sound devices are added tools of cohesion and coherence rather than the primary tools.

111

Poets, however, can learn much about sound devices from lyrics and from songwriters. Primary sound devices to be explored in this chapter include prosody, alliteration and assonance, cacophony, and euphony. Why are sound devices so important? They are not just pretty (euphonious) or ugly (cacophonous), lovely or harsh to the ear; the very content of them produces a tone; tone conveys meaning.

Think of the movie *Jaws*, for instance, without the musical score or the thumping sound that preceded a death strike. Sound can produce fear, quell fear, or move us to sorrow and tears.

Perhaps this is a good place to suggest that poetry students avoid writing poems with specific meter and exact end rhyme. Leave that for years ahead after the basics have been mastered. The problem is if poets use meter, it must be impeccable and controlled; if poets use end rhyme, it must be impeccable and controlled. In our experience, emerging writers struggle with this.

Poetry with meter and rhyme problems can sound at best like singsong greeting-card verse or a Poe poem imitation and at worst amateurish and awkward. Our advice is to avoid specific meter and exact end rhyme for now. But this chapter will offer an introduction to some primary meters such as iambic pentameter and show us how the strongest poets use and manipulate end rhyme.

On the other hand, meter and rhythm exist inherently in lines of poetry as the language itself, the very syntax, initiates its own rhythm. Syllables, repeated consonant sounds, produce a type of meter when read aloud or spoken in the mind. There are types of rhyme such as repeated vowel sounds (assonance) that produce internal rhyme; there are words that are not exact rhymes but near or slant rhymes, as Emily Dickinson called them.

Finally, the way the poem looks on the page and the way the poet handles the number of lines per stanza and stanza usage in general contribute to how sound is used and managed in any poem. Dickinson's poem "After Great Pain" uses all of these elements of prosody and sound devices. There's no alternative poem option for this chapter.

TERMS USED IN THIS CHAPTER

Alliteration: One of several important sound devices, and related to assonance. Alliteration is the repetition of consonant sounds, particularly at the beginning of words, as in "as she fleeth afore / Fainting I follow" ("Whoso List to Hunt" by Thomas Wyatt).

Assonance: Assonance means the repetition of vowel sounds as in v*o*wel s*o*unds. Lyrics, particularly country-western lyrics, rely on assonant rhyme. Poets use this device primarily for internal rhyme, as in Dylan Thomas's "Grave men near death who see with blinding sight / Blind eyes could blaze like meteors and be gay, / Rage, rage against the dying of the light." The repeated long *a* and long *i* sounds in that phrasing serve the poem as a sound and tonal device.

Cacophony: Cacophony and euphony are also related sound terms, cacophony implying a harsh and unpleasant sound and euphony implying a beautiful and pleasant sound. A good example of cacophony is the line "I woke to the black flak of the nightmare fighters" in Randall Jarrell's "Death of the Ball Turret Gunner"; note how the *black flak* assonance and alliteration sound like and remind the reader of the onomatopoeic *ack ack ack* sound of machine gun and anti-aircraft gunfire.

In contrast, euphony is expressed in words with flowing sounds and repeated letters of pleasing consonant and vowel sounds. Walt Whitman is a master of this, as in the lines "I saw in Louisiana a Live Oak growing" and "When lilacs last in the dooryard bloomed." Repetition and wordplay such as this line from Gerard Manley Hopkins's "I caught this morning morning's minion, king / dom of daylight's dauphin, dapple-dawn-drawn falcon" and this use of anaphora by Robert Hayden are good examples of euphony: "What did I know? What did I know?"

Meter: Meter involves the beat, the rhythm of the line. As poet Mary Oliver says, "Rhythm underlies everything" (43). Students of poetry may find it helpful to think of the musical beat of any song. Most poetry employs accentual meter rather than syllabic meter, but both can be used to create the meter of any poem or poetic line.

Iambic pentameter, which some have suggested is closest to the rhythm of the human voice, is one example: "Is *this* / a *dag* / ger *which* / I *see* / be*fore* me?" or "She was / a *wo* / man *love* / ly *in* / her *bones* / When *small* / birds *sighed* / she *would* / sigh *back* / at *them*." Note the clear five beats (pentameter).

Prosody: As persona encompasses all parts of the narrator/speaker, so too does prosody encompass all parts of rhythm and rhyme in any poem, including meter, rhythm, accent, alliteration, assonance, and any other sound devices. (It is pronounced "prah'–zi–dy.")

Rhyme: Rhyme or rime means the similarity of sounds in words used together for effect. Simply put, nursery rhymes frequently use end rhyme, as in "Peter Peter pumpkin *eater*, had a wife and couldn't *keep her*" (imperfect rhyme, assonant rhyme) and "There was an old woman who lived in a *shoe*, she had so many children she didn't know what to *do*" (near rhyme) and "Tyger, Tyger, burning *bright* / In the forests of the *Night*" (perfect masculine rhyme).

THE MODEL POEM

After Great Pain

by Emily Dickinson

After great pain, a formal feeling comes
The Nerves sit ceremonious, like Tombs—
The stiff Heart questions was it He, that bore,
And Yesterday, or Centuries before?

The Feet, mechanical, go round—
A Wooden way
Of Ground, or Air, or Ought—
Regardless grown,
A Quartz contentment, like a stone—

This is the Hour of Lead—
Remembered, if outlived,
As Freezing persons recollect the Snow—
First—Chill—then Stupor—then the letting go—

THE EXPLICATION

Miss Dickinson is the ideal poet to use here because this masterful poem illustrates all of the craft devices studied in previous chapters as well as presenting us with a model of a poet's fine ear for prosody and sound devices. This poem deals with the stages of grief and healing following the loss of a loved one. It seems to presage Kübler-Ross in understanding that grief indeed has stages. Dickinson finds three: the initial pain of the blow, the utter stupor of despair and loss, and finally the blessing of "letting go."

First, it is important to note that the speaker is a tightly controlled person of a philosophical nature who speaks in clipped phrasings, perhaps as a way of controlling emotions that might otherwise overwhelm. The phrasing, as musicians call it, is distinctive; those dashes surely are breaths, sighs almost. Imagine the speaker in your mind. Imagine how the voice would sound, how the phrases would be delivered.

Note how this poem—a fixed form—sits on the page: three stanzas, though of unequal line length. The second stanza makes its own way, rebellious of form and meter, as Dickinson is wont to do. Dickinson knows all the elements of poetry, punctuation, and sound and uses them impeccably or breaks them at will.

She preferred the use of dashes to commas, periods, and semicolons or other punctuation; she uses capital letters in unusual places. Indeed, she surprises us with her freedom of thought and her disregard for rules. The odd second stanza seems to suggest to readers on first glance that something is amiss. Even that is a valuable lesson for students of poetry. How a poem looks on the page influences readers too and can complement and supplement a poem's content and meaning.

First, let's examine the stanzas for end rhyme. "Comes" and "Tombs" are inexact rhymes or slant rhymes, but they work together to create a cohesion of sound; "bore" and "before" are exact rhymes, though the first masculine and the second feminine. "Round" and "ought" repeat the assonant "ou" followed by the rhyme of "grown" and "stone" at the end of lines 8 and 9.

The final stanza offers the off-rhymed "lead" and "outlived" with the exact rhyme of "snow" and "go." The final masculine rhyme with its hard and heavy one beat seems to underscore the hardness of reality in the poem's topic and theme.

Dickinson shows us how to play with end rhyme in an individual and fresh way. Also, she uses internal rhyme, that is, slant rhymes usually produced by assonance or vowel repetition in places other than end-line words, such as "nerves" paired with "ceremonious" ("er" and "er"), the "ou" sound of "Ought" midline, "regardless" and "Quartz" with its repeated "ar" sound.

Note how such sound work creates cohesion between and among words and lines, tightening the text, showing enormous control.

The poem's rhyme scheme can thus be established as AA, BB, CC, DD, EE, FF. Now let's listen to the meter of each line. *"Af'ter great pain'*, a *for'mal feel'ing comes.'"* Each italicization indicates an emphasis or a beat. Note that beats in meter are not necessarily related to syllables; they can be but need not be. There are five beats to this line; five beats equals pentameter. The accent of "after" is debatable: It could be heard as an equal meter *Af'ter'* (a spondee). For example, stanza 1 reads entirely in pentameter and, moreover, in iambic pentameter:

> The *stiff* Heart *ques*tions *was* it *He*, that *bore*,
> And *Yes*ter*day*, or *Cen*turies be*fore?*

Iambic means the stress or accent falls on the second metrical "foot," which may be a word or syllable, as in "He *ran*, he *fell*, he *rose* another *day*." Pentameter means five beats to the line. Repeat those lines until you hear the five-beat rhythm with accented words and/or syllables. But as Dickinson prefers variation, she does not sustain this perfect iambic pentameter throughout the poem.

She does not return to it until the final two lines of the poem. In stanza 2, the lines retreat into a rigid, military, or hymnal kind of meter and rhythm, which seems to accent the loss of control a person feels in such a situation of loss and grief. Listen to the music of these lines:

The **Feet**, me**chan**ical, go **round**—	(4 beats) Tetrameter
A **Wood**en way	(2 beats) Dimeter
Of **Ground**, or **Air**, or **Ought**—	(3 beats) Trimeter
Re**gard**less **grown**,	(2 beats) Dimeter
A **Quartz** con**tent**ment, **like** a **stone**—	(4 beats) Tetrameter

However, lines 2 and 4 of this stanza go together meaningfully; thus, the stanza's meter reads 4, 2, 3, 2, 4. The meter stumbles just like the person stumbles after a great loss. This is a special kind of genius.

In lines 10 and 11, as in stanza 2, Dickinson uses trimeter (three beats to the line). In this shift from the more "normal" rhythm of language, which, as Shakespeare declared, seems to be naturally an iambic pentameter, stanza 2 and half of stanza 3 are out of step, as if knocked askew until the healing begins in the final couplet, which again picks up the iambic pentameter. See, then, how sound and prosody can accent, contribute to, and even control feeling and meaning? Ideally, as Frost said, sound and sense are one.

Original	Paraphrase
After great pain, a formal feeling comes	*After something terrible happens, our emotions become formal and*
The Nerves sit ceremonious, like Tombs—	*cold,*
The stiff Heart questions was it He, that bore,	*Our now-hard hearts ask if our suffering is akin to Jesus's? (Our*
And Yesterday, or Centuries before?	*suffering hearts are compared to Christ.)*
The Feet, mechanical, go round—	*We keep moving, robot-like, un-*
A Wooden way	*aware of our surroundings, until*
Of Ground, or Air, or Ought—	*the pain changes to numbness, a*
Regardless grown,	*weird oblivion, as if our hearts*
A Quartz contentment, like a stone—	*and souls have turned to stone.*
This is the Hour of Lead—	*This is the worst moment, one we*
Remembered, if outlived,	*will remember if we make it*
As Freezing persons recollect the Snow—	*through*
First—Chill—then Stupor—then the letting go—	*Like people who nearly die remember their peril: the pain, the nothingness, the healing that begins with forgetting.*

Notice the words that produce cacophony or unpleasant sounds that seem to capture the emotional content Dickinson wants to deliver with them, such as "stiff" heart, "mechanical" feet, the "Hour of Lead," the words "chill" and "stupor." In contrast, the euphonious sound of "letting go" conveys a sigh of relief.

Other words convey meaning through their sound too, like gloomy "Tombs" and the odd word "Nerves." The entire phrase "The Nerves sit ceremonious, like Tombs" uses both personification and simile. That phrase and the word choice of "ceremonious" suggest that people go through the formalities of death at funerals and wakes, politely bearing up, speaking in euphemisms and listening to platitudes.

Dickinson's phrasing also personifies our emotional selves, our "Nerves sit" and our "stiff" hearts question. These phrasings and use of sound devices create startling imagery.

The major metaphor of the poem is in the final stanza: "This is the Hour of Lead." With this choice both in sound and sense, Dickinson offers her interpretation of what such a passage through pain and stupor *feels like*. It feels like lead weight on our souls, an unbearable pressure. She shifts then to a leap of sorts, another simile: This hour of lead is "Remembered, if outlived, / As Freezing persons recollect the snow."

If we survive this loss and the agony of spirit that follows, if we endure, we will remember only some of it, the wild whiteness of pain and the utter steel cold of oblivion, the hours or days or months of endurance. We will begin to forget, and we will forget; that is the blessing and the healing.

This poem teaches us so much about the artful choice and use of language tools; it is a culmination of all the previous chapters' learning plus a lesson in sound and sense. It is an example of a mighty poet using her honed tools of craft to create a masterpiece.

EXERCISES FOR STUDENTS

Quick Exercise 1. Sounds (15 minutes)

For fifteen minutes, brainstorm two lists of words: one that is full of cacophonous (inharmonious) sounds and one that is rich with euphonious (harmonious) sounds. Consider the words for both meaning (denotative and connotative definitions) and sound qualities. Reflect on the list or share it with others when the exercise is done. Use what you have learned here in the model exercise for this chapter.

Quick Exercise 2. Hearing and Creating Meter (15 minutes)

Using the examples on the preceding pages regarding meter (dimeter, trimeter, and tetrameter), brainstorm a list of words and phrases for each one. Remember that rhythm and meter are not necessarily syllabic. Try several. Really work at hearing and creating meter in your phrasings. Consider using meter in your upcoming poem.

THE MODEL EXERCISE

Write a poem in three stanzas about some kind of a loss you have endured and survived. If you wish to write about someone else's loss and not your own, that is okay too. You can use this same theme without rhyme and meter as well; see student Marcy Sieradzki's sample poem at chapter's end about a doctor going in to convey terrible news to a patient.

If grief or loss is too much for you to tackle right now, try this optional assignment: Write a poem in several stanzas with or without rhyme or specific meter that uses sound as a specific device to show meaning. Note Ariane Anderson's poem, "Beneficent Echo," in the student poems at chapter's end, for example.

Create a fixed-form poem with an end rhyme pattern of AA, BB, CC, DD, EE, FF. Strive for iambic pentameter; escape into the freedom of another meter if it works in the poem meaningfully. Use slant and perfect rhyme; use masculine (one syllable) and feminine (two or more syllables) rhyme. Internally, strive for words that create meaningful assonance and alliteration.

Two of the stanzas should be quatrains; one can be a variation (or not, as you wish). In this poem, pay particular attention to your word choices vis-à-vis their sound value: How does the sound contribute to the meaning you want to convey? Concentrate on choosing every word with care and an ear attuned to sound as meaning. Remember previous exercises using imagery, metaphor, and line endings and marry them here to sound.

Create at least one metaphor. This is important: Ask yourself, what does grief feel like? Smell like? Sound like? Can it be personified in some creative way? Create at least one simile. Use strong imagery line by line. Avoid telling how you feel. Show feelings only through sound and imagery.

SAMPLE STUDENT POEMS

Beneficent Echo

by Ariane Anderson

Jacob concerto suspended.
Saffron prismatic early light
splayed on Cathedral floor.
Modernist plaintive strains
are muted. Dissonant chords gather, tightly constrained,
horn "rips" strings swell
piano crescendos.

Cadenza flows purposefully, effortlessly,
through rhythmic circles of virile articulation.
Controlled singing pulls taut, then collapses.
Frozen flashback of
child sitting on gymnasium floor
hearing Beethoven's pastoral horn.
Mighty swell enfolds burnished memories.
Notes painting genius on imagined surfaces.
Sanctified breath, binary effusion.
Viscerally push . . . retard . . . exhale . . . sing . . .
pray.

Patient Waiting

by Marcy Sieradzki

He hesitates, sighs, his gaze
falls on the doorknob's smooth surface
polished by rivers of fingertips.
She is waiting.
His heart drums staccato beats—
crescendo, allegro, ears throbbing.
A dry swallow.
She is waiting.
It never changes, it never will.
The crisp white of his coat

offers no hope.
She is waiting.
Desperate, even as the cool metal steals
warmth from his hand.
Desperate, even as the cruel cells steal
life from her body.
She is waiting.
Nothing left but a click, turn,
displaced air,
and her expectant inhalation.

Over Exposed Film

by Ashley LaRose

His eyes hung low always staring
at the tiny black monkey that fell off his back
and now guides him through his day. It seems
on Tuesdays such as this, the waft of Giorgio
Armani gives off a metal taste as it presses
the rewind button in my memory.

REFERENCE

Oliver, Mary. *A Poetry Handbook: A Prose Guide to Understanding and Writing Poetry*. San Diego, CA: Harcourt Inc., 1994.

Chapter Eleven

Punctuation

A Surprisingly Creative Tool

Your first discipline is your vocabulary; then your grammar and your punctuation.

—Robert Frost

Creative writing texts rarely have a chapter discussing punctuation. Maybe that is because people tend to take punctuation for granted. In a poem, it is the punctuation that clues the reader how exactly to read the poem, where to pause, where to stop for a moment, where to stop for more than a moment, when to read quickly down the page, and so on. Punctuation serves the reader much like line endings and techniques like caesura and enjambment. Punctuation marks are road signs to the reader.

Sometimes a writer will run a poem down the page with no punctuation other than line breaks. This does work sometimes when a poet is extremely good with line breaks and the reader learns early on in the poem that the poem is read line by line without very much direction; however, this style of writing is often not successful because the reader gets lost in the poem and the poem loses meaning in the process.

Often emerging writers fall into the trap of writing poems with little or no punctuation, partly because they may think punctuation isn't as important to the poem as it is. They think a line break is sufficient to let the reader know how they are supposed to read the poem, when to pause, when to speed up, and so forth. It's not possible to pace a poem well without punctuation, as how else do we control the sound, the emotion, the delivery of phrasing?

Sometimes the absence of punctuation and grammar works to make a poem, but such usage must be deliberate. The more experience a poet has at learning how to pace a poem and use punctuation deftly, the better the poem will be.

Lola Haskins's poem "Grandmother Speaks of the Old Country" illustrates all the devices discussed in the book so far with an emphasis on the artistry of punctuation.

TERMS USED IN THIS CHAPTER

Punctuation: The use of Standard English marks that indicate pauses and full stops, including but not limited to commas, semicolons, colons, dashes, ellipses, hyphens, and periods.

Repetition, Parallel Structure, and Anaphora: The deliberate use of repeating a phrase, word, or clause to draw attention to its intent, sound, and/or meaning. A perfect example is the closing couplet of Robert Hayden's modern sonnet "Those Winter Sundays," in which he writes, "What did I know, what did I know . . . ," with the implied variations of emphasis and meaning in the repeated same words. Poets can use simple repetition of words for effect; they can use parallel structuring of stanzas, ideas, and images for effect; and they can use anaphora for effect. Anaphora should be used deftly and with an ear for tone and meaning; anaphora has the effect of conveying a powerfully emotional tone to the reader, as in the Hayden poem, where the anaphoric line sounds like bells tolling.

THE MODEL POEM

Grandmother Speaks of the Old Country

by Lola Haskins

That year there were many deaths in the village.
Germs flew like angels from one house to the next
and every family gave up its own. Mothers
died at their mending. Children fell at school.
Of three hundred twenty, there were eleven left.

Then, quietly, the sun set on a day when no one
died. And the angels whispered among themselves.
And that evening, as he sat on the stone steps,
your grandfather felt a small wind on his neck
when all the trees were still. And he would tell us
always, how he had felt that night, on the skin
of his own neck, the angels, passing.

THE EXPLICATION

In her poem "Grandmother Speaks of the Old Country" Lola Haskins
allows the voice of this grandmother to tell the harrowing story of death
passing through a small village. Haskins's use of punctuation throughout
the poem enlightens the reader of just how powerful punctuation can be.
One might say that punctuation is an ordinary craft tool, but it can also
perform extraordinary tasks.

The first line of the poem is a simple sentence with a period at the end
of the line, so there appears to be nothing special here; however, it provides the ominous entrance into a poem about "many deaths." It ends with
the word "village" with a solid pause for the period, the next line begins
with the word "germs." The pause links the village to the germs with a
capital G. These are large, deadly germs that amazingly fly "like angels
from one house to the next."

Haskins links the worldly germs with the otherworldly angels, as if
God has a hand in the fact that "every family gave up its own." The word
"mothers" stands alone at the end of line 3 and is a terminal caesura. This
places emphasis on the word "mothers," and the reader suspects the next
line will be disturbing at the very least.

Because the line is enjambed, the reader moves quickly on to the next
line, where these mothers "died at their mending." Mothers are the nurturing keepers of the keys of the hearth, and Haskins deliberately shows their
demise first in order to show just how relentless the germs are. The fourth
line basically breaks into two equal parts, a medial caesura, with a period
at the end of this sentence and at the end of the line—two end-stopped
lines to give them equal importance. First the mothers die and then the
children fall "at school."

Haskins is very careful with her punctuation here, making sure to convey a feeling of loss equally to the mothers and the children. The imagery is particularly powerful as well: We see the dying of the mothers and children like frames of an old film. "Mothers died at their mending. / Children fell at school." The brevity of the sentences, the simplicity of delivery, the simple verb choices all effectively contribute to the horror.

The poem moves from this medial caesura to the exact number of lost children by showing the reader how many survived: "Of three hundred twenty, there were eleven left." Haskins places this information on one end-stopped line so that the reader has ample time to digest this distinct feeling of terrible loss.

Next Haskins ushers in a "quiet" turn of events as the sun sets on "a day when no one / died." Notice how Haskins enjambs the line and ends the sentence on the next line using an initial caesura. She places the emphasis on "died," but in this case "no one / died." The enjambment urges the reader on to the next line, which ends the sentence abruptly. Haskins takes advantage of the many ways one can use the poetic device of caesura.

After ending the line abruptly with the word "died," Haskins goes on with a short sentence that ends this line. "And the angels whispered among themselves." Here the poem's tone changes like a breeze blowing in; the verb is "whispered." The entire poem so far seems a recollection of a dim drama of hopelessness against disease; sentences are short. Phrasing is clipped. All this intensifies the dying. But here, the reader senses a shift.

The angels have such power over life and death that this story hearkens back to the biblical story where the Jews had to place blood on their front door so that the angel of death would pass over their home and not take away the life of their firstborn. The angels whisper on the morning no one dies; the reader feels the tragedy must have passed. There is hope that perhaps God has called his angels home. Like the "small wind on his neck" felt by her husband, readers hear the angels whisper and feel them pass.

Haskins now turns the poem away from death and describes the grandfather sitting on the stone steps where he feels "a small wind on his neck / when all the trees were still." There is something mystifying about this wind, since the air is still. And now we come to the last sentence in the poem, fraught with commas—pauses—chills. The sentence is enjambed twice, so the reader scans it quickly, yet the commas make sure that the reader pauses on each phrase where Haskins wants a breath.

"And he would tell us / always, how he had felt that night, on the skin / of his own neck, the angels, passing." Notice how Haskins enjambs the beginning phrase so the reader quickly reads "always" on the next line, but then she uses a comma to create a pause on "always." She has the next phrase with a comma before "on the skin" and then another enjambed line, so "of his own neck" is read quickly, but then another comma where she says "the angels" comma "passing," leaving the poem with an emphasis on passing. This is a beautifully rendered sentence.

Haskins uses parallel structure and repetition here as well, in the repeated phrasings—not quite akin—of "on his neck" and "on the skin of his own neck." Note the power of that repetition and phrasing; it is elegiac and mystical.

This particular poem is a study of punctuation from beginning to end. Haskins's artistry with punctuation and use of poetic devices such as enjambment and caesura can be seen throughout. The final sentence, which encompasses three lines, is a study in itself. As the speaker in the poem, the grandmother is utterly believable, her language ordinary, yet Haskins's deft ear makes it come alive with poetic grace.

EXERCISES FOR STUDENTS

Quick Exercise 1. Learning to Be Critically Reflective (15 minutes)

Take a look at your portfolio of poems right now. Select two. Spend ten minutes reading and reflecting on these poems and consider how punctuation is used in them. Using a pen or pencil, perhaps a highlighter too, mark parts that could use better, more deliberate punctuation. Considering what you have learned from the Haskins poem, how might you use punctuation more effectively in the poems?

Look at the common punctuation marks like periods and commas. Could you use another kind of mark here and there? Would a colon work somewhere? How about a semicolon instead of a period? If you have too many lines with end punctuation, consider rewording them using enjambment. Have you used caesura? If not, is there a spot where caesura would be effective to fully pause the reader at a spot in the poem, a place to reinforce meaning?

Quick Exercise 2. Editing and Revision for Stronger Punctuation (20+ minutes)

Now using the two poems you selected and marked above, spend ten minutes on each one, revising and editing your punctuation. Try using punctuation choices you rarely use, like the dash, for example. A dash looks like this—and differs markedly from the hyphen, which looks like - . The dash indicates a longer pause than a comma, a moment for the reader to reflect on what came before. Make sure your use of punctuation, spacing, and line endings is deliberate and artful.

THE MODEL EXERCISE

Option A. Write a new poem of similar stanzas, line breaks, and punctuation to the Haskins model poem. Find your subject matter in an anecdote someone in your own family has told over and over again. Or ask a grandparent or older relative to recount a family story. Listen to their words; watch their body language. In a notebook, take notes. Then make that person the speaker of your poem. The trick is to keep the voice ordinary, normal.

Your diction choices should capture the way the person delivers language; the pacing should capture its meaning. The voice needs to be honest. Listen and write. Listen from your heart.

From this point on in your writing, realize the importance of punctuation and the wondrous tools of the craft. They are like an artist's paintbrushes, each with a deft and different stroke and intention.

Do not use exclamation marks. Keep the action underplayed, as does Haskins. Make sure there is a shift in tone—a significant shift in tone—somewhere toward the end.

Option B. Revise the poem or both poems you selected for quick exercises 1 and 2. Retype them. Put the new draft(s) into your portfolio. Spend some time thinking about the changes you made and why you made them. What have you learned about using punctuation effectively? Write one paragraph in answer and place this in your portfolio along with the drafts of your poem(s).

SAMPLE STUDENT POEMS

Eagle Pine

by Richard VanWagner

for mom

My memories are often dusted
with the unrelated. Such is JFK's death
powdered with the sound of snapping sheets
on an afternoon New England line.
As the taste of dark toast unbuttered dry
will always be sprinkled with the crumblings of September 11th,
so my mother's cancered death coated
my cold late-winter walks by eagle pine.

In chore there I grew still as she passed,
the stealthy flash of her winged perfection
countering the cries she hurled out and down.
Cries that I, brim back would catch
until my eyes turned up, would burn,
and I would be forced to swallow—or drown.

In this time I knew she'd tip her fluid grace
to right—to light,
finding her evergreen embrace with ease
while I below damp kneed the grass
until my neck ached
and chest ceased to heave.
Listening, as echoes of her settled peace

were seized by sudden calls of liberty
that would tumble out on my shoulders
as prayers flew past—
then they were no more.

It's been three springs now
since my mother took flight.
Yet she coasted in this year
with two brindled young at her side,
their pitched voices lifting up and out
filling my empty chest pocket.
And in the stillness of their rest,
as the winds of a new season were dusted
with the quiet chaff of taloned bark,
I found my hope renewed—
forever boughed in the heart of eagle pine.

Orchestrating Slumber

by Lacey Varnum Autry

The sun yawns,
It's time.
On tip-toes I grab one of his beams
and tug.
Resistance.
Then submission.
The descent begins. I point forcefully at the mountain. It separates
into two peaks and gently cradles
the sun's body between them.
Watch.
Closely.
I gesture to the mountain's deciduous daughters. They bend
forward their branches and softly stroke
the sun's forehead with velvet leaves.
Look.
Closer.
I cue the sacred river's entrance. It births
a lullaby as it pushes and forces

itself over smooth stones in its path.
Listen.
Listen.
I shush the tiny flowers as they beg
for their friends' speedy return with peaceful
assurance
same time
tomorrow.
I step into the wind. It whispers
and coos sweet nothings while it lifts me up
to kiss the warm face
of its child.
Sleep. My love.
Sleep.

NOTE

Credit: Lola Haskins, "Grandmother Speaks of the Old Country." Reprinted by permission of Lola Haskins.

Chapter Twelve

Effective Titles

Hints at Theme

Each has his past shut in him like the leaves of a book known to him
by his heart, and his friends can only read the title.

—Virginia Woolf

In poetry classes, emerging writers seem at a loss regarding titles of their
work. Many poems are submitted for workshopping without titles or
called "Untitled." That's a little like placing the word *Untitled* at the bottom
of a great painting. Titles embody energy and carry the power of the
theme into the beginning of a poem. Titles can be thematic, directly or
indirectly. Good titles connect the readers to the poem.

Sometimes the title will begin the poem and serve as its first line.
Sometimes the title will place the poem in time and space, serving to
move the contents forward, as in Mr. Kooser's postcard-like title "January
19 / Still thawing, breezy." In a way, titles can offer backstory.

When learning to write, we don't want our poems to become mysteries
to the reader. We want to share our meaningful experience and guide
readers to what we're after in the poem. For this reason, it may be the best
advice to tell poets to create titles that are literal and directive. We don't
mean call the poem "The Tree" if you write about some kind of philosophic
conversation written under and inspired by some tree; that would
be simplistic. But literal, concrete, that's another thing.

Think of some titles by great poets. How about "The Windhover" by
Gerard Manley Hopkins? Nothing to guess at there. Or another poem by
Hopkins, "Pied Beauty"? That title is both literal and interpretative. These
are the kinds of titles to strive for in writing poetry.

Titles can be powerful things that lead poems to sharing their intention and their theme with readers effectively. Look back over the poems studied so far in this book; imagine any one of them without a title or with a different title. For example, what if Wilbur had named his poem "First Snow in Alsace" "Untitled" instead?

What if Frost had called "Out, Out" instead "Vermont in the Distance"? It is easy to see that such different titles affect the quality of meaning and lead readers to meaning.

This chapter then offers model poems that use titles in various ways and show a variety of title techniques.

Jean Valentine in her book *The River at Wolf* includes a poem titled "We Go Through Our Mother's Things." A close look at the poem reveals the significance of the title. A second model poem in this chapter, "Strawberries" by W. S. Merwin, shows us the power of a well-titled poem.

THE MODEL POEM A

We Go Through Our Mother's Things

by Jean Valentine

When we started that day
to paint snow for earth
and sky for bread
then we knew it was time to light the last candle.
This ring is yours. This lamp.

THE EXPLICATION

The reader enters the poem through the title, "We Go Through Our Mother's Things." A good title is one that leads toward meaning in any poem. One can picture a group of two or more siblings gathered round and looking through their mother's belongings. The assumption is that the mother has passed away and the siblings have the job of going through her things, discarding what is not wanted and then distributing the remaining items.

The title becomes essential to the meaning of the poem. Without the title, the reader has nothing to hang on to when reading the next three lines of the poem. The title becomes a meaningful line in the poem itself.

Now the actions truly begin with the following image: "When we started that day / to paint snow for earth / and sky for bread / then we knew it was time to light the last candle." Valentine uses the surreal images to attempt to capture the unreality of losing a parent. How does one translate painting snow for earth and sky for bread? This is not an easy task. Like a blanket of white, snow covers the earth in cold.

Snow symbolizes the coldness that surrounds someone who has lost a loved one. The expanse of sky above has no color, but the unending nature of the heavens, the speaker's unwillingness to accept her mother's admittance into heaven, changes into the nurturing nature of bread.

The reader imagines that Valentine's relationship to her mother was strong and fulfilling; therefore the loss of that energy in her life is almost impossible for her to accept. The speaker gives the reader a glimpse of the level of grief she experiences by her need to change snow/cold into mother earth and sky/heaven into daily bread.

Now Valentine says, "then we knew it was time to light the last candle." The reader knows this candle represents grief and the letting go of the mother. This ritual softens the loss somehow. Valentine uses few words in this poem, so every word seems to count twice.

Valentine ends the poem with two short statements on the same line, a type of anaphora with its use of repetition for effect. In this poem, the last line sounds both childlike (this is mine, that is yours!) and elegiac (mournful, dirge-like): "This ring is yours. This lamp." How do these siblings decide to whom to give what item? Is there a list left somewhere that delineates the mother's wishes?

Did she tell them before she died? No, it seems they are left to parcel her things out, to go through her things one by one, to decide who gets what, and to make peace with her dying in this exercise of grieving.

There lies the beauty of Valentine's work. With just a few lines down through the poem, she describes the strange consciousness involved with the loss of a parent and the process the siblings go through. Her strange, surreal images suggest that a person's mind conjures up unreality in order

to come to terms with such a great loss. Her ending suggests the true nature of loss as the parent's belongings are dispersed and removed from the
home where they have perhaps spent a lifetime.

The title, of course, is essential in this particular short poem. How
would the reader recognize what goes on in this poem without the title?
Without this title, which is, in fact, the action of the whole poem, there
would be no way for the reader to enter the poem. The title informs
the reader that the family gathers together to go through their mother's
things.

Valentine knows exactly what she is doing. She does not want this
poem to be in any way sentimental. She avoids this by reducing the information to the bare bones of the experience. She adds no extra words or
phrases, but rather reduces the poem by having a title that carries a great
deal of weight.

This title enables Valentine to get right to her point and then end
quickly. Poets can learn so much from this brief poem about the power
of striking imagery and the creation of a strong title that leads the readers
into the poem itself. Should a poet create such titles all the time? No. But
it is a surprise when this happens. Keep that in mind.

THE MODEL POEM B

Strawberries

by W. S. Merwin

When my father died I saw   a narrow valley

it looked as though it began   across the river
from the landing where he was born   but there was no river
I was hoeing the sand   of a small vegetable plot
for my mother   in deepening twilight
and looked up in time   to see a farm wagon
dry and gray   horse already hidden
and no driver   going into the valley
carrying a casket

and another wagon
coming out of the valley   behind a gray horse
with a boy driving   and a high load
of two kinds of berries   one of them strawberries

that night when I slept   I dreamed of things
wrong in the house   all of them signs
the water of the shower   running brackish
and an insect of a kind   I had seen him kill
climbing around   the walls of his bathroom
up in the morning   I stopped on the stairs
my mother was awake   already and asked me
if I wanted a shower   before breakfast
and for breakfast she said   we have strawberries.

THE EXPLICATION

Merwin serves up a delicious poem, complex, lonely, foreboding, and mysterious, yet he gives it a seemingly simple title, "Strawberries." Strawberries come to symbolize so many levels of meaning here: the suggestion of high summer and the boy's youth and vigor, the red stain of a wound, the way life suggests sometimes, particularly in traumatic moments, a pattern as does this poem.

The poem itself exemplifies every craft tool and artful sensibility this book has discussed. Even the shape of it on the page serves the poem because it is an unusual pattern, one that defies logic and reason, maze-like, cohesive, like a path leading us from title to image to foreboding image to conclusion. The title is ironic in its simplicity, implying in the end a gravitas terrible and magnificent. The speaker is a boy hoeing in the garden, who with his sensibilities enhanced in some mysterious fashion notices things that twilight in a way unusual.

The poem lists these things and uses spaces and spacings and stanzas to do so. Merwin rejects standard punctuation in this poem as if to suggest it is a poem about something so unusual, some kind of magical synchronicity and portent, it deserves no borders and no boundaries. Yet, even in its formlessness, the pattern connects from line to enjambed line, from twilight to dawn, from foreboding to actuality.

EXERCISES FOR STUDENTS

Quick Exercise 1. Reflecting on Titles (10 minutes)

Brainstorm a list of titles from poems you know. You can also use titles of books and films if you like. You might include titles of artworks like Van Gogh's "Starry Night," DaVinci's "Adoration of the Magi" or "The Last Supper," or Paul Monet's "Impression, Sunrise." Choose five. Decide which title is the "best" from among those on your list. Ask yourself why. Defend your choice when the group discusses this exercise. In your mind, be thinking about your own poetry titles. Were they strong and fitting? How so or how not?

Quick Exercise 2. Titles First! (10 minutes)

Think of five strong lines that are both image and action, such as "We go through our mother's things." Perhaps it is something like "We Watch My Little Brother Pitch His First Game" or "I Stand Vigil at Grandmother's Bedside." Put them down on the page and just study them. Try a few and settle on your favorite line. Reflect on how you might continue a poem from the title you wrote. If you have time, go ahead and write a few lines that would follow this title. The end line could follow Valentine's structure of repetition.

Quick Exercise 3. Creating Titles (10 minutes)

Write a quick poem. That's right. Just like that. Pick one of the titles from quick exercise 2 above and let it spur you into writing the poem itself. Lay down the images fearlessly. Don't think too much. Share it with someone (a peer, a friend, a member of your poetry workshop if you have one) and ask others to guess the title. Think about their suggestions. From the feedback, consider revising your poem and title.

THE MODEL EXERCISE

Both model poems illustrate the value of a well-chosen title. Each title serves the poem in a unique way.

Option A. Continuing from the in-class quick exercises and using the Valentine poem as a model, finish the poem you began in exercise 2 above. Let the title place the reader in time and space; let the title suggest the depth of meaning and lure the reader in. You want to intrigue your reader with a title. You want that reader moving eagerly from title to poem.

Note how the well-chosen title packed with information saves any possible editorializing and needless wording. Now the speaker can plunge directly into the action, fearlessly.

Try to keep this poem short, five lines in length. It is a free-form poem, with only an inner rhythm to guide it. Note the lines on the page are of varying lengths.

Dare to lay down the action as Valentine does: How did the action begin? What tone was set by the action? Let the final line convey the action and suggest the depth of emotion held back by the use of understatement. Give it two parts, two sentences phrased a similar way.

Option B. Using Merwin's poem as an example, write a poem about an odd dream or the death of someone you loved; connect the dream and/or the death with food somehow, possibly one food in particular, as Merwin does using "strawberries."

Use the poem as a model to write about the death of a person you knew and loved (or hated or even did not know well—it could be a neighbor, a stranger, a homeless person—as long as you connected with that experience in a powerful way). Brainstorm a list of images from the night and morning of the day this death happened. Use the open, free-form poetic structure, yet connect your images in an underlying, cohesive manner.

Your title word must be the primary cohesive device, as it is in the Merwin poem. Maybe in your case it is crape myrtle or carrots peeled in the sink or a fat moon low on the horizon. Whatever it was, as you recall it, it was a portent of kind; it was as you view it now, foreboding. Weave that wonder and imagery through your poem. Use the title word at least three significant and well-chosen times, including the title and the last word.

SAMPLE STUDENT POEMS

2:54 A.M.

by Melissa Bussinger

Neon blue numbers blink at me
through eyes glued shut. Time
ticks away. The pulsing cadence
changing my heartbeat.

The fan blades swing dangerously
in their effort to catch each other.
None gains the lead in their frantic race
which could end with the flick of a switch.

Night sweeps regrets onto my doorstep.
Staying well past their welcome, invading
my bed, pushing sleep past the lump
in my heart to sour in the pit of my stomach.

I lie awake, forget my dreams,
accept the new reality.
I push it all down
and hope they haven't awakened the others.

A Different Kind of Book Burning

by Chris Shaber

Lying in bed, reading about
the mysterious submariner
surrounded by the words of long dead
authors, he is at peace. The door crashes

open and the giant stumbles into the room
smelling of hops and barley. A calloused hand
yanks the boy out of bed. "Get outside
and clean the yard!" he slurs.

Stifling sobs, the boy picks up sticks
for the burn barrel, watches the giant
lumber from the house with all his treasures.
As they tumble into the fire, one by one,

he can hear Sher-Khan roar in fury, Sewell's horse
whinny in terror and the young boy from Missouri
scream as the flames curl the edges and black
out the words, devouring them without mercy.

NOTES

Credit: "Strawberries" by W. S. Merwin. Copyright © 1997 by W. S. Merwin, used by permission of The Wylie Agency LLC.

Credit: Jean Valentine, "We Go Through Our Mother's Things" from *The River at Wolf*. Copyright © 1992 by Jean Valentine. Reprinted with the permission of The Permissions Company, Inc., on behalf of Alice James Books, www. alicejamesbooks.org.

Chapter Thirteen

Nature as Muse

There was a time when meadow, grove, and stream,
The earth, and every common sight,
To me did seem
Apparell'd in celestial light . . .

> —from "Ode: Intimations on Immortality from
> Recollections of Early Childhood" by William Wordsworth

Many things prompt the muse, such as love, heartache, loss, a specific person, our pets, our memories, our relatives, stories we have heard, places we have lived. One inspiration poets have called on throughout the ages is nature itself, which can inspire by its beauty or harshness, its raw power, its delicate fragrance; simply sitting in one spot and witnessing nature can help us begin a poem in time and space and lay down initial images in any poem.

In an earlier chapter, we mentioned the concept of muse and noted it throughout the book in a number of places. The concept of muse means a "guiding voice." Sometimes nature can do more than help us create vivid imagery; it can suggest metaphors and serve as symbols, as in the Richard Wilbur poem "First Snow in Alsace," for example, that propel the poem toward meaning or connect idea to thing, showing readers what a poet is after.

Robert Frost, for one, has been called a nature poet, though he is much more than that, of course. Nonetheless, even his titles suggest nature served as muse. One of his earliest books of poems was titled *North of Boston*; that book is rich with poems of place and setting, gardens, farmyards, brooks, and birds. We recommend it as a book rich with poems about place, landscape, and nature.

It has been our experience that more often than not, emerging writers do not think enough about setting, place, landscape, or nature itself. These things are noticeably absent from their work; adding them improves their work.

So how does nature inspire us as a muse? Writers can find a spot and focus their attention. Poets can notice the sensory devices evident; they can jot down the concrete images, particularly ones that are unique, things the average person might miss. Then poets can ask themselves, image by image, *what is this thing like?* What does it remind me of in real life? What kind of human situation might I compare to this image in nature?

"Traveling through the Dark" by William Stafford is a poem inspired by an encounter with nature. Here, the speaker is rather darkly critical of humankind and in a post-transcendental way sees a geometry of heaven, God, and his purposes through observations of nature. We have chosen it as our sample poem for this chapter.

Stafford uses his difficult choice with the deer to symbolize the kinds of hard choices we make on this road of life, and he tells us, let there be no swerving from what must be done. Such poems show us how becoming a good witness of the world around us, the world of animals and wild things, can serve as muse.

TERMS USED IN THIS CHAPTER

Transcendentalism (and Post-Transcendentalism as we use it): Transcendentalism is a broad term to define. Briefly, it was a mid-nineteenth-century American movement in theology, philosophy, and literature that espoused the ideas of God as an oversoul and nature as illustrative of God's purposes. Its tenets involve a broader and deeper understanding of God than the harsh, Calvinistic concepts of early New England settlers' faith.

Its followers were fiercely independent thinkers and forward-thinking idealists, such as Ralph Waldo Emerson, Henry David Thoreau, Bronson Alcott, Margaret Fuller, and arguably Nathaniel Hawthorne.

To some extent, it could be said that Emily Dickinson and Walt Whitman too were Transcendentalists who rejected form and rules and narrow theologies. This freedom of thought and independent spirit transcended the past in American thought and theology.

THE MODEL POEM

Traveling through the Dark

by William Stafford

Traveling through the dark I found a deer
dead on the edge of the Wilson River road.
It is usually best to roll them into the canyon:
that road is narrow; to swerve might make more dead.

by glow of the tail-light I stumbled back of the car
and stood by the heap, a doe, a recent killing;
she had stiffened already, almost cold.
I dragged her off; she was large in the belly.

My fingers touching her side brought me the reason—
her side was warm; her fawn lay there waiting,
alive, still, never to be born.
Beside that mountain road I hesitated.

The car aimed ahead its lowered parking lights;
under the hood purred the steady engine.
I stood in the glare of the warm exhaust turning red;
around our group I could hear the wilderness listen.

I thought hard for us all—my only swerving—
then pushed her over the edge into the river.

THE EXPLICATION

Stafford's poem shocks us and leaves us with hard truths. There is little mercy to be found in it, only an implicit tenderness. Note how the situation is that a female deer, a pregnant doe, has been killed by a car on

the side of a dark, rural road in "the wilderness." The tone of the poem
is altogether foreboding; the "group" is not defined, but somehow the
speaker is its leader and decision maker. The imagery seems deliberately
imprecise. He writes

> I stood in the glare of the warm exhaust turning red;
> around our group I could hear the wilderness listen.
> I thought hard for us all . . . (Lines 15–17)

Nature itself leans in and listens, he suggests; it is a living thing, the wilderness. It is alert and watching us, conscious of our choices, nodding in
approval or shaking its head in disapproval.

The speaker keeps tight control of his words just as the poet keeps
tight control of his fixed-form poem in its multiple quatrains and ending
couplet. The poet keeps the reins taut as if to suggest two things: The first
is that if we allow emotion, we will fail in our duty to do the hard right
things required of us in this world; and secondly the poem itself is so full
of misery, it is unbearable to allow emotion. Thus we must keep tight
control. And so he does.

Stafford lays the poem on the page in controlled stanzas. He employs
enjambment and caesura to pace his poem, to ensure his readers pause
and listen where he wants them to pause and listen, particularly in the
seventeenth line with his double use of the dash, which serves the poem
as it shows the harsh decision, the pausing, and the action.

> I thought hard for us all—my only swerving—
> then pushed her over the edge into the river. (Lines 17–18)

The speaker's voice here is that of a father: children, turn your heads
and walk away now. This is all we can do; this is the only choice. In other
places in the poem, the speaker warns us of the harsh choices we must
make, choices that seem already made in our collective conscience: "It is
usually best to roll them into the canyon" because "to swerve might make
more dead."

This road, "Wilson River road," which hints at a road of life, has its
perils and its griefs and its hard mercies. One can barely say what happens
here, this pushing of a live fawn off the cliff because it is doomed, this

act that must be done to protect other cars and travelers, and that shortens the fawn's suffering.

With this poem in its casual diction, told as one would convey an anecdote by firelight with a glass of wine, leaning forward, *here is what happened* . . . , Stafford confronts his responsibility as a humane and responsible person in the hard world. We never quite forget the speaker's hand on the side of the doe where it feels the fawn lying "there waiting, / alive, still, never to be born." This line too implies all our losses, things never brought to fruition, hard choices made out of duty and love and experience.

EXERCISES FOR STUDENTS

Quick Exercise 1. Generating Ideas (10 to 15 minutes)

For this poem, brainstorm a few experiences you have had with animals in the wild (not tame pets; a zoo animal might work). From that list, create a cluster of details and images you recall from memory. Let some time pass. Choose the best topic with the most vivid imagery and strongest, most unusual details.

Quick Exercise 2. Organizing Ideas (10 to 15 minutes)

From the list generated in exercise 1, begin to organize your details and images into two stanzas that will become two separate parts of your poem. Decide what will happen in stanza 1 and what will happen in stanza 2. Try dividing your poem into a description of the situation in 1 and what happens in the end in 2. Think about them as two separate but related poems about one animal.

THE MODEL EXERCISE

Using the quick exercises as your impetus, write a poem about an unusual experience you had with a wild creature of some kind. See the poem by student Ethan Marcus Goode in chapter 7, for example, about a wild bird he had rescued and then decides to free.

In your poem, make a conscious effort to include and illustrate your worldview, using the encounter with a wild creature as your venue. This is an exercise in critical reflection and philosophical conclusion as well as just writing about nature. Make sure your focus in the poem is specific and detailed rather than broad and general.

Stretch your philosophical self to draw an important conclusion about life and death from the critical reflection and epiphanies (if any) you have while examining this situation and writing this poem.

The epiphany may strike you midpoem, so don't expect to know what you think until you begin to write. Writing leads to such discoveries; trust the process of writing to lead you to truths.

By this point, you know how to lay down the poem in images, line by line; you have some practice in paying attention to line endings and last words on a line; you can use punctuation or the lack of it to serve the poem. You have experience searching for apt metaphors and using poetic devices of sound and sense. Since this is an advanced chapter in the book, we expect it will draw on everything you have learned so far and more than that—push you to new heights and competence.

When you are finished with your poem, let it sit a while (a few days is best). Read it aloud to someone. Ask for their honest feedback. Let them read it too before answering. Go back and prune, prune, prune. Get rid of extraneous words and weak verbs.

Delete adjectives and adverbs if you can reword with an action or stronger verb imagery. Adverbs are particularly "telling"; use them rarely. Adjectives are fine, even simple ones like color, size, or shape, but don't smother the poem in them.

Make sure your speaker is the right one to tell the story and convey the poem. Shift to second person you/your midpoem and speak directly to readers. Ask yourself, what did this animal's action or experience, life or death, teach me? What did I learn from it? How did it validate or invalidate what I believe or used to believe was true about being in the world?

These are tough questions, yes. It's time. You're ready. Title your poem something powerful and something that suggests an underlying connection between humans and beasts.

SAMPLE STUDENT POEMS

Barn Owls

by Marcy Sieradzki

We stood together, mother's arm draped
over small shoulders for warmth,
breathless, ears buzzing with silence.

A spill of mercury moonlight cast crisp
shadows of aged oaks reaching down
to bathe in the silver-dewed grass.

Though unseen, I could picture them,
small white faces like halved apples,
gliding through darkness on vapor wings;

their presence revealed by unrepressed
chortles like children huddled
under a blanket, giggling with joy.

Soon their voices drift further away,
off to regale other midnight creatures
with strains of their singsong laughter.

He looks up at me, brilliant smile laced
with traces of enchantment lingering,
revealing the evening's hidden story:

his own little apple face, and in his eyes
silent wings budding, waiting to carry him
quietly away to places I'll not know,

leaving me to stand alone, breathless
in my own twilight, straining to remember
the sound of his childhood refrains.

For Charlotte

by Frank Hukill

Nothing like Hollywood has scared us
though definitely not a pageant winner
some of your cousins are sort of . . . pretty
almost, like an artist's drop cloth.
Colored like a camouflaged soldier
you do not draw out my urge to pet
I stand and marvel at your skill
of weaving, child of Arachne

As if to clean for company
you glide down one side of your web
living drop of condensation
on a glass of summered ice tea

Inspection of your strands reveals
a minor flaw you quickly mend
this corner of my shed your home
will be until you spin no more.

My Kingdom

by Chris Shaber

Tucked behind 31st Street was my forest kingdom
not a large kingdom but mine.
Pillars of oak and pine dwarfed me
as I explored its verdant halls.

The giant door set on the ground, hinting
at a subterranean world peopled with orcs, trolls and elves.
An old Pontiac, rusted, missing its wheels and doors
with a tree growing up through the engine compartment.

Life abounded all around me
slithering, scuttling, scurrying, singing.

Perched in trees in multihued glory.
Dashing under ferns in grey-brown streaks.

It
was
not
a
large
kingdom
but mine.

NOTE

Credit: William Stafford, "Traveling through the Dark" from *Ask Me: 100 Essential Poems*. Copyright © 1962, 2014 by William Stafford and the Estate of William Stafford. Reprinted with the permission of The Permissions Company, Inc. on behalf of Graywolf Press, Minneapolis, Minnesota, www.graywolfpress.org.

Chapter Fourteen

The Prose Poem

A Revelatory Form

> Which of us has not, on his ambitious days, dreamed up the miracle of
> a poetic prose, musical without rhythm or rhyme?
>
> —Charles Baudelaire

Many readers wonder why prose poems are called prose poems at all.
Indeed they are nothing more than narratives (at least usually), more often
than not a fairly short piece of prose telling a story, an anecdote, in poetic
prose. Given this fact, how does one define a prose poem or what makes
it a poem and not a short piece of prose? The distinction between "poem"
and "prose poem" can be the prose-type line endings.

The only thing clear is that it's often difficult to define a prose poem
or to tell one from a regular poem. There are "fictional" or story-like elements in a prose poem that make it somewhat different from a "regular"
poem (although some—if not all, some would argue—tell mini-stories).
Another thing that sets the prose poem separate from the regular poem is
its revelation. Revelation serves as its primary device.

No doubt, there is an unclear line between prose poetry and a paragraph
of prose. But one could define it this way: *A prose poem seeks to share
some truth or revelation in a brief paragraph of prose that uses poetic devices.* The line ending is gone. The words, the images, the revelation must
convey meaning. Editing and pruning become the most important tools in
addition to initial selection of words, phrases, and imagery.

Some say that the prose poem pays more attention to the language than
to the musical rhythm. Others say there is a bit of short fiction and poetry
in a prose poem. David Caplan in *Poetic Form* says the prose poem was

created as an escape from the traditional alexandrine twelve-syllable line (226). Caplan identifies three kinds of prose poems: a short narrative, a short prose piece that imposes its own linguistic or literary rules, and a two-paragraph prose poem frequently alluding to or using myths or fables while at the same time avoiding their "sanctimoniousness, the paternalistic moralism" (228).

However, when viewed on the page, a prose poem seems easy enough to identify as distinguishable from either a "regular" poem or a short short story. It is generally one paragraph, though some employ two. It is brief and uses a choice of poetic devices. Most are revelatory in some fashion of a truth about human experience. Most importantly, it can be an interesting form to write, freeing poets from some of the poetic constraints of line endings and opening up the poetic form to prose qualities.

TERMS USED IN THIS CHAPTER

Narrative: A mode of composition that intends to tell a story or retell an anecdote about experience.

Prose Poem: A paragraph or number of paragraphs written in poetic-type language with prosody and including attention to details such as imagery, metaphors, and other types of figurative language. It is a blend of prose and poetry; its quest is a revelation of truth.

Short Short Fiction: Fiction from three hundred to one thousand words that tells a story as briefly as possible for narrative effect; currently, it is also termed flash fiction. The difference between flash fiction and prose poetry is arguable, but prose poems use poetic devices while flash fiction does not rely upon them.

THE MODEL POEM A

Adolescence

by Nin Andrews

The winter her body no longer fit, walking felt like swimming in blue jeans and a flannel shirt. Everything stuck to her skin: gum wrappers,

Band-Aids, leaves. How she envied the other girls, especially the kind who turned into birds. They were the ones boys hand-tamed, training them to eat crumbs from their open palms or to sing on cue. What she would have done for a red crest and a sharp beak, for a little square of blue sky to enter her like wings. But it was her role to sink so the others could rise, hers to sleep so the others could dance. If only her legs weren't too sodden to lift, if only her buttons would unfasten in the water she kept swimming through, and she could extract from the shadow of her breasts a soul as soft as a silk brassiere, beautiful and useless, like a castle at the bottom of the sea.

THE EXPLICATION

This prose poem offers several revelations in its meager 155 words. The first is that the speaker is bitter and creative; the second is that nothing she says is literal. Why would things like leaves and gum wrappers "stick" to her? How could the other girls turn "into birds"?

The third is she has to realize that some people are blessed with beauty and popularity; it's their job in life, so to speak, whereas those unfortunates like herself are meant "to sink" in comparison "so the others could rise . . . sleep so the others could dance." This is nonsense, of course, but in this language of abstraction and imagery resides a young girl whose adolescence was so painful it still throbs. The prose poem hums with it.

In the opening line, the speaker says, "The winter her body no longer fit, walking felt like swimming in blue jeans and a flannel shirt. . . ." To imagine "her body no longer fit" seems an apt description of how this adolescent feels about all the changes going on in her body. Puberty is such a difficult time for young girls, and Andrews manages to capture this change in a few short words—one small image.

The fact that Andrews chose winter and not spring for this occasion is interesting to note, as one would think she would choose spring; however, that would be the more obvious choice. By selecting winter instead, Andrews suggests that adolescence is almost like hibernation, actually that point of coming out of hibernation, when everything begins to wake up. It's not spring yet, but rather just at the point where the bulbs underneath the ground begin to turn their heads upward. That may be its fifth revelation.

The speaker is having a difficult time adjusting to this dramatic change in her life. For her, the world leaps out to catch her arms and legs; everything seems to weigh her down, like the image of her in jeans in the water. She's not able to take this change in stride like some of the other girls.

They seem to glow with it, grow with it, so much so that they are transformed into birds, those creatures who can fly around the heavens, and nothing sticks to them, certainly not the wind around them, or the things of the world. They have the ability to somehow escape ugly and uncomfortable adolescence, to a point.

Later readers see that these are the girls who themselves become caught, birds in a game where boys win and boys control it all. So, the speaker suggests, the transition of young girls—whether those who are birds or those who are not—from adolescents to women is uncomfortable and difficult.

The speaker says these girls are "the ones boys hand-tamed, training them to eat crumbs from their open palms or to sing on cue." We hear resentment in those words. The speaker begins to distance herself from such trained "creatures" like those other girls. She's different; she's not like them, not only in looks but in character. She will not be like those girls, ever.

The truth of the matter comes out. This young woman sees the way the social world expects girls to behave: trained and tamed, for one thing. And even worse, to take whatever little scraps the boys offer them as if this is all they are worth. Notice how the writer conveys this with one good image of trained birds in 155 words. It shows us something about prose poems; be economical with language, but be clever and precise.

Oddly enough, adolescence has pulled this girl spiraling downward into the sea, being pulled under by the weight of her jeans and flannel shirt. She seems to be drowning. Rather than being up in the sky, spiritually in tune with the nature of the in-crowd, flying like a bird, being beautiful and trained to amuse boys, she is wishing she could find her "soul" somewhere inside between her breasts, "a soul as soft as silk" that should by rights give her hope that if she does find it, then she will be freed.

But this is not the case. Her soul will be useless, as the "castle [is] at the bottom of the sea."

This poem is about the disappointment for so many young girls at this age, and ironically Andrews connects the disappointment with the sky, heaven, and the beautiful soul of the girl. Even her soul would be useless if she were to find it. It is ironic that a girl so young and beautiful sees herself in such a negative light. It is a foolish truth she endures and with which she makes herself miserable.

Looking back at this prose poem as a whole, it does read like a poem, even though it certainly doesn't look like a poem on the page. Andrews manages to make quite a statement about adolescence in this brief poem. She titles it concretely and unambiguously.

The second example of a prose poem is an untitled poem by Gary Young. It is curious why Young chose not to title his poem. Some artists simply do not title their work, leaving what might be a serious call of attention to the word or phrase lost to the reader. Perhaps they are afraid the title will distract from the poem. Most poets, however, feel that the title adds to the overall poem and offers the reader even more meaning.

THE MODEL POEM B

Untitled

by Gary Young

I discovered a journal in the children's ward, and read, I'm a mother, my little boy has cancer. Further on, a girl has written, this is my nineteenth operation. She says, sometimes it's easier to write than to talk, and I'm so afraid. She's offered me a page in the book. My son is sleeping in the room next door. This afternoon, I held my whole weight to his body while a doctor drove needles deep into his leg. My son screamed, Daddy, they're hurting me, don't let them hurt me, make them stop. I want to write, how brave you are, but I need a little courage of my own, so I write, forgive me, I know I let them hurt you, please don't worry. If I have to, I can do it again.

THE EXPLICATION

This 135-word prose poem is a painful, haunting portrait of the father of a very ill child. There is great courage in this poem as well as sadness. Without any sentimentality whatsoever, the speaker conveys the unspeakable.

The speaker finds and reads a journal in the waiting room of a children's hospital. We know it's serious business; this kind of hospital specializes in critically ill, fatally ill, children. Parents, children, whoever wants to, all are allowed to jot down their thoughts or feelings.

Listen to how it reveals its truths in one paragraph.

The poem begins with the father saying that "I discovered a journal in the children's ward, and read, I'm a mother, my little boy has cancer." Already there is a tone of sadness in the poem, a sense of loss of control of life. The mother's words in the journal don't say that she has lost control of her little boy's life, but the reader has a sense of this feeling anyway.

She just makes a straightforward comment: "my little boy has cancer." That comment is enough to evoke feeling in the reader. Another writer, a patient, says she has had nineteen operations, a seemingly infinite type of suffering.

Notice the author gives us no description of the scene here. There is no picture of the hallway, the flooring, the lights, the numbers of children up and struggling or those lying in bed. The reader has the barest of information to go on here, yet as the poem continues, it turns out to be quite enough.

The speaker says, "She's offered me a page in the book. My son is sleeping in the room next door. This afternoon, I held my whole weight to his body while the doctor drove needles deep into his leg." The scene begins to sharpen with this image of the father. Now we know the man is a father and his son is on the children's ward too; readers know the struggle between the doctor, the father, and the son.

It is a forced struggle in that the father has to hold down his own son in order for the doctor to treat the son. The language here is significant. The speaker says that the doctor "drove needles deep into his [the boy's] leg." The verb choice of "drove" with no hint of mercy or crying shows us just how merciless this situation is and just how much strength and courage are required by the boy and by his father.

Here is the hardest image, the one that conveys what kind of guts it takes to be the parent of a terribly ill child. You have to be the kind of parent who can hold down his child so that the doctor can drive the needles deep into the child's leg. You must be the kind of parent with the courage and the strength to lean your "whole weight" against the child's body.

It is the choice of this one detail, this one image, that creates the power of this poem. Like the image of birds in the previous poem conveyed both beauty and stupidity, frailty even, the image of the father leaning all his weight to hold his child down so that the doctors can hurt the child in their quest to heal the child, is the only one that would convey the whole truth.

So. The revelation is another harsh one, something akin to Jeffers's worldview in "Hurt Hawks." Sometimes in life situations demand from us more than we imagine we can do or bear; we rise to them or we don't. Nobody else can do it; no mercy steps in to help. Or perhaps, says Young, the mercy, the only mercy is in the parent's fortitude to hold on, to hold down, and to keep trying.

The father finishes up his entry in the journal by saying, "I want to write, how brave you are, but I need a little courage of my own, so I write, forgive me, I know I let them hurt you, please don't worry. If I have to, I can do it again." This is a stunning and surprising ending. All along, the reader was wondering what this father was feeling and what he might write in this journal.

Virtually, he says, I'll do it again—hold my child down so that doctors can try to heal him, no matter the pain, no matter how much my child cries and begs for me to let up and for them to stop.

The few details Young offers in this poem are enough to create this prose poem that leaves us rocking.

EXERCISES FOR STUDENTS

Quick Exercise 1. Writing a Prose Description (15 minutes)

From wherever you are sitting, write a one-paragraph prose description of your environment. Use all the tools you have been learning throughout the book, chapter by chapter. Capture all types of sensory data as you construct unique imagery. Do not line your writing as a poem but let it flow as a prose paragraph. Share it with the class. Count your words. Keep it under two hundred words.

Quick Exercise 2. Writing a Second Prose Description (15 minutes)

Write a second prose paragraph with the same basic directions as the first above. This time, write from your imagination, not from reality. Pick a memory; set it in time and place. Be careful not to cover too much territory in time and place. Best to stick to narrow parameters.

Ask yourself: Why did I choose this scene? What happened there/here that changed me? Write it down as a narrative. Think about your point of view and your speaker. Add more detail about how this moment in time changed you. This is an added epiphany to a simple narrative paragraph. Share these prose paragraphs with the class.

THE MODEL EXERCISE

Write two prose poems in which you consciously create no deliberate line endings and allow the poem to create a natural paragraph form. Each one must be approximately 150 words. In it, tell a story, briefly and imagistically, about the experience or situation. In the first, model your prose poem on model poem A, which focuses on adolescence or the end of childhood.

In the second, narrate an incident of illness you remember regarding yourself or another person that was significant and meaningful to you. In both, seek to find the truth of the experience; trust the revelation of your own muse.

In the first, select an awkward moment in your youth, or select a moment when you seemed to slip from childhood into adolescence. Maybe it was a summer's day when you found you could no longer go shirtless; maybe it was a winter's afternoon when you first saw peach fuzz on your upper lip. Prose poems move much like fiction in that they have a narrative plot line, if brief, that has climax and denouement.

In the second, plumb your memory for a time when someone was ill. It could be yourself or someone close to you. Perhaps it is a brother or sister, a cousin, a grandparent. Remember how you felt at that time. Choose a particular scenario such as a bedside or a hospital room. As you write, use the poetic tools of craft, the figurative devices, you have learned in this book.

Choose your speaker with care and deliberation. Even if the experience happened to you, personally, consider the best choice of point of view. Perhaps you could tell the truth of this experience better from the cool territory of third-person perspective. It's up to you.

Pluck images from your memory moment that share emotion with the reader, that emphasize the dilemma of the situation. Use some colors in this poem. Let us hear the rustle of the bedsheets, smell the fetid air of the dark bedroom.

Seek the revelation of that dilemma: What really happened to you, inside? What did this time in your life mean to you? What truth was revealed to you at that moment? Title your poem or leave it untitled.

ALTERNATE MODEL EXERCISE

For students who struggle with the above exercises or those who want to write more prose poems, try this one, using a photograph. Find a photograph from your personal life that speaks to you. Use it as the inspiration for your prose poem. Set the photo's contents down in images: Color? Landscape? Shapes? Shadings? When? Where? Try using a few well-chosen proper nouns like St. Cloud or Uncle Paul.

Look below the surface of the photo and relate its "story": Why does it intrigue you? What does it say about the world? Of course, your job is to show these truths, not to tell them. Don't editorialize in any way. Select rich descriptive imagery.

As above, seek a word content of 150 to 200 words. Prune 20 percent. Kill your darlings. Scan the photo with the poem on a single page to share with others.

SAMPLE STUDENT POEMS

The Wrinkle
from Trilogy of Age by Melissa Bussinger

The wrinkle carved out the valleys of time across her face, telling more than any doctor's note. Her hands, once soft in all the right places and rough from work in the others, now looked like derelict ship sails hastily torn down; the salty air left them to bake in the hot sun. They weren't her hands, no matter how long she looked at them. These hands had felt so many second chances, yet they still want more. She had always been so careful when she was younger, a rebel in words only, the actions always coming up short. It chilled her to think of her own children going through this one day. Would they recognize their own failing features? Their once prized looks gone to waste, all for nothing. What had her looks gotten her anyway, besides trouble? Her children had supplied her with a framed picture of her in her nurse's uniform from when she was in her twenties. Its only purpose was for the chubby assisted care helper to look at wistfully and comment on how beautiful she had once been.

Plague Harvest

by Kristin Pressey Schulkers

Summer was swollen with the promise of flies. In my loneliness, I sought him where dying earth met the clotted sky. Rejected by grace, we picked our way through shattered melodies, the bitter wreckage of our own disaster—dream, as thunder shared its secrets of anger and loss. In my languid fever-trance, I turned and watched the stars fall from his eyes. I dissolved myself in the acid-bath of his tears, and, fading, found redemption in distance, my lost horizon crushing ever inward, infinitely smaller than it was the night before. The notes of our discord flowed unevenly over the open mouths of self-inflicted wounds.

NOTES

Credit: Nin Andrews, "Adolescence" from *Why They Grew Wings*. Reprinted by permission of Silverfish Review Press.

Credit: Gary Young, "I discovered a journal in the children's ward" from *Even So: New and Selected Poems*. Copyright © 2012 by Gary Young. Reprinted with the permission of The Permissions Company, Inc., on behalf of behalf of White Pine Press, www.whitepine.org.

REFERENCES

Caplan, David. *Poetic Form: An Introduction*. New York: Pearson Longman Publishers, 2007.

Chapter Fifteen

Writing in Various Forms

I'd sooner write free verse as play tennis with the net down.

—Robert Frost

The exercises and assignments in the previous chapters have dealt with poetry that employed free and fixed forms. Chapter by chapter, some attention has been paid to learning about stanzas of varying lengths and lines of various rhythms and rhyme patterns. So the groundwork for learning traditional fixed forms has been laid.

This chapter is different in a couple of important ways. First, it is the final chapter containing lessons and sample poems. It would be quite easy to spend two weeks or two classes on this chapter's assignments alone. Secondly, the chapter—while introducing traditional form—is not meant to be conclusive or an in-depth study of them. Rather, it is a culminating chapter, bringing together all tools and sensibilities and experiences from the fourteen previous chapters.

Chapter 15 differs also in that there are no explications of the poem samples but rather a brief description and summary of the sample types and poems.

The sample poems are meant to be read aloud and discussed as a group. We hope you will read them aloud and talk about them—how do they work? What makes each interesting? What kind of subject matter might work with what kind of fixed form? The form should serve the subject matter, no question about it.

Though it isn't critical that poets know how to write in traditional forms, it is part of the accepted pedagogy of art that we study what has been done before and learn from it. A piano student learns from Brahms and Bach, Mozart and Chopin; he goes on to play in a jazz band! Finally, this chapter serves as a closing and a bridge—a closing to the book and summary of all things learned in it as well as a bridge to the next step, the advanced levels of writing poetry.

Sometimes writing a poem using a form forces the writer to "pound the poem into shape," as Anne Sexton once said about writing in forms, and this kind of poetry requires the use of rhyme, meter, structure, and so on. There are prerequisites. There are rules. It can be fun, and it can be a learning experience.

Writing in fixed forms enables a modern writer to have a strong foundation to work from when entering the world of poetry. Forms allow the writer to experience many different styles of writing, which builds the foundation of craft possibilities for the young poet.

Most importantly, poets shouldn't be intimidated by fixed forms, including rhyme, meter, stanza types, and prosody. Note the student poems included at the chapter's end. Many students took right to fixed forms; their work blossomed to new levels of competence, poise, composition, and merit. Try some; you never know. You just might like them!

TERMS USED IN THIS CHAPTER

Elegy: A type of poem in which the dead are honored and sometimes spoken to directly by the speaker.

Free Verse: Any poem not of fixed forms; a poem of no particular form or meter but one that has elements of prosody nonetheless.

Haiku: Traditionally, haiku involves creating a poem using twenty-one syllables, striking images, and three lines in a one-stanza poem. The form is credited to the Japanese.

Sonnet (Modern and Shakespearean): A fixed form consisting of a fourteen-line poem with a defined rhyme scheme, either the ABBA ABBA CDDC EE or the Elizabethan sonnet or the traditional Italian ABAB CDCD EFEF GG (or variation thereof). The sonnet has a time signature of five beats to the line or iambic pentameter. Think of

Shakespeare's heroes and antiheroes saying things like "Is this a dagger which I see before me?" Note the meter of the line, Is THIS a DAGger WHICH I SEE beFORE me? (five stressed beats) or "To BE or NOT to BE, that IS the QUEStion."

Sestina: A fixed-form poem from the French and Italian poets of the late Middle Ages and the Renaissance based on six-line stanzas or sestets in which six words chosen by the poet are repeated in order throughout the poem's stanzas. The sestina has thirty-nine lines, six sestets as explained above plus an ending of three lines called an "envoy," where all six words are repeated in a particular order.

Villanelle: A nineteen-line French fixed form comprised of five tercets and one quatrain where lines 1 and 3 are repeated throughout and the poem ends in a couplet of repeated lines 1 and 3.

SONNETS

The two sonnet examples are both Elizabethan variants of the sonnet. The rhyme scheme of the two sonnets below is listed at the end of each line. Traditional sonnets are written in iambic pentameter, a five-beat line beginning with an unaccented word or syllable (the iamb) followed by an accented syllable or word: - / - / - / - / - / . Or one might write this five beats to the line rhythm as: *da dah da dah da dah da dah da dah.*

THE MODEL SONNET A

Sonnet 130

by William Shakespeare

My mistress' eyes are nothing like the sun;	A
Coral is far more red than her lips' red;	B
If snow be white, why then her breasts are dun;	A
If hairs be wires, black wires grow on her head.	B

I have seen roses damask'd, red and white,	C
But no such roses see I in her cheeks;	D
And in some perfumes is there more delight	C
Than in the breath that from my mistress reeks.	D
I love to hear her speak, yet will I know	E
That music hath a far more pleasing sound;	F
I grant I never saw a goddess go;	E
My mistress, when she walks, treads on the ground.	F
And yet, by heaven, I think my love as rare	G
As any she belied with false compare.	G

THE MODEL SONNET B

Whoso List to Hunt

by Sir Thomas Wyatt

Whoso list to hunt, I know where is a hind	A
But as for me, alas, I may no more,	B
The vain travail hath wearied me so sore;	B
I am of them that furthest come behind.	A
Yet may I by no means my wearied mind	A
Draw from the deer; but as she fleeth afore	B
Fainting I follow; I leave off therefore,	B
Since in a net I seek to hold the wind.	A
Who list her hunt, I put him out of doubt	C
As well as I, may spend his time in vain!	D
And graven with diamonds in letters plain,	D
There is written her fair neck round about;	C

'Noli me tangere; for Cæsar's I am,   E

And wild for to hold, though I seem tame.'   E

THE VILLANELLE

As complex as the sestina is the villanelle, a fixed form comprised of six stanzas, including five tercets and one quatrain, with a rhyme scheme of ABA and a deliberate repetition of lines of 1 and 3 throughout and in the end couplet.

Obviously, it is a complex and beautiful form when mastered. Dylan Thomas's poem is the most frequently anthologized villanelle in English poetry. Note its prosody and graceful movement from line to line and stanza to stanza. Thomas repeats lines 1 and 3 so deftly and logically that readers have to look closely to note the rhyme scheme.

THE MODEL VILLANELLE

Do Not Go Gentle into That Good Night

by Dylan Thomas

Do not go gentle into that good night,	A	Line 1
Old age should burn and rave at close of day;	B	
Rage, rage against the dying of the light.	A	Line 3
Though wise men at their end know dark is right,	A	
Because their words had forked no lightning they	B	
Do not go gentle into that good night.	A	Line 1
Good men, the last wave by, crying how bright	A	
Their frail deeds might have danced in a green bay,	B	
Rage, rage against the dying of the light.	A	Line 3
Wild men who caught and sang the sun in flight,	A	
And learn, too late, they grieved it on its way,	B	

Do not go gentle into that good night.	A	Line 1
Grave men, near death, who see with blinding sight	A	
Blind eyes could blaze like meteors and be gay,	B	
Rage, rage against the dying of the light.	A	Line 3
And you, my father, there on the sad height	A	
Curse, bless, me now with your fierce tears, I pray.	B	
Do not go gentle into that good night.	A	Line 1
Rage, rage against the dying of the light.	A	Line 3

EXERCISES FOR STUDENTS

Quick Exercise 1. (1 hour; 30 minutes to prepare, 30 minutes for students to present)

Pick any poem in this textbook that has not been discussed in class yet and spend fifteen minutes identifying its rhyme scheme, its rhythm, and any specific fixed-form devices that it employs.

Ask yourself, why did the poet choose to use these devices? Why did the poet choose a free over a fixed form? Many poems are a combination of free and fixed forms or loose-form poems. Answer the question. Share your answers. Students might want to "teach" their poem using a blackboard or computer screen.

Quick Exercise 2. (20 minutes)

Construct lines 1 and 3 of a villanelle you might write. Use Dylan Thomas's poem "Do Not Go Gentle into That Good Night" as your guide. Try to come up with several groups of lines 1 and 3. Choose the best lines. Share them with the group.

Make sure lines 1 and 3 are powerful, alliterative, rich in meaning, and worth repeating throughout a completed villanelle. Write the lines on the board or share on a computer screen for maximum impact. What have you learned about how lines work together? What is similar about the end couplet of a sonnet and repeated lines 1 and 3 of the villanelle?

THE MODEL EXERCISE

Write one fixed-form poem (select from the following):

1. Write a modern-day sonnet, using contemporary language to express the lover's dilemma in Sir Thomas Wyatt's mournful "Whoso List to Hunt." Line by line, rewrite the sonnet in your own language, using slang and any current diction that seems appropriate to you. Maybe you could use text writing, for example, to abbreviate words and make the sonnet and situation truly contemporary. Try to re-create the rhyme scheme or a slant rhyme scheme.

2. Write a villanelle. Make sure to follow the rhyme scheme and repetitions required of lines 1 and 3 throughout and couple them at the end. Try to make the repeated lines sound logical and graceful. The repetition of lines 1 and 3 should form a powerful couplet in the final quatrain. One anonymous young student's first villanelle was called "Center Ice," and it used ice hockey as its conceit:

Line 1: Now here we are at center ice;

Line 2: This frozen lake's the strangest vice.

It was funny, serious, an interplay of whimsy and real life. It was the student's best poem of the semester. Our point: Don't be afraid of the villanelle! If you can find two lines that bear repeating, that can be restated a number of times for multiple, complex meanings, you may have a fine poem in the making.

SAMPLE STUDENT POEMS

Sonnets

Last Year's Day

by Marcy Sieradzki

I watch the merriment through sleepy eyes,
Crowds gathered underneath a diamond sphere.
As fireworks blaze in velvet skies,
A joyous throng sings praise to the new year.

Old follies left behind, they sing instead
Of wisdom gained through time and revelation.
All eyes fixed on the joys that lie ahead,
And opportunities at reparation.
Yet at the gala's end all that remains
Are visions of grey sky and fresh-turned earth
My ears remember requiem refrains;
No thoughts of sweet redemption or rebirth.
For this day at death's harrowing behest
We laid you (just eighteen) to your last rest.

Cheating on Life

by Hannah Ferguson

Lie with me, Sleep; pull me down to the dark and deep.
Cradle me closely in your surreal abyss.
Touch me, taste me with your strange, lipless kiss.
Free me, capture me and into my mind creep,
As my forgotten body in the night gropes and weeps
For something created by anything other than this
Voice of yours in my dream's ear you hiss.
Oh saturate my being, but be kind to me, Sleep.
When our rendezvous is come to an end
And we are caught—discovered by the waking dawn—
We will have to be more careful the next day . . .
Come, Sleep, from Life I have stolen again,
And he will never know that I am gone
Unless, that is we get carried away.

Villanelle

God's Sweet Gifts of Days[1]

by Rick Metcalf

Do not sleep late into the daylight hours
Nor fritter idly God's sweet gifts of days
So much to do in this short life of ours

No, rise before the sunlight tips the towers
Before the meadows sense its warming rays
Do not sleep late into the daylight hours

Unlike the sloth as yet in bed he cowers
Who squanders costly time and still delays
So much to do in this short life of ours

He has no time to stop and smell the flowers
"I don't have time to do a thing," he says
Do not sleep late into the daylight hours

Those moments that a lazy man devours
Are lost, however strongly he inveighs
So much to do in this short life of ours

Before that youthful dynamism sours
Too late to mend such languid drowsy ways
Do not sleep late into the daylight hours
So much to do in this short life of ours.

Quatrain in Iambic Pentameter

Northbound Moon

by Rick Metcalf

A half-thousand mile trek northward begs a story
Some piquant morsel gleaned from yesterdays
And grandma laughs mid-phrase as she recounts it
My nose pressed flat against the limpid pane.

Tall redwoods in an upside-down armada
Sail swiftly by our car on either side
Wakeless in a blue-grey, waveless ocean
Whose fish with wings swim impudently near.

Tall sails dim into eerie long-armed phantoms
All grasping for the sequined cape above

Their never-ending battle rages southward
The rushing moon fades in and out of view.

Then sequin-stars evolve to velvet blackness
Her stories blur into a jumbled muse
Until half-dreaming as the door squeaks open
I hear her whisper, Ah, we're finally home.

Rhymed One-Stanza Poem

11:37 on 3rd and Broadway

by Richard VanWagner

On her lips a mote of bitter
melted curvy sweet.
A touch for token barter
betraying those who cheat.
Armed in ruptured tangles
of breath and merging beat.
Her supple knap of nettles
bowing men before her feet.
Scenting their ill begotten
they fall in full retreat.
From her eyes, a painted given.
From her soul, the lonely street.

NOTES

Credit: By Dylan Thomas, from *The Poems of Dylan Thomas*, copyright ©1952 by Dylan Thomas. Reprinted by permission of New Directions Publishing Corp.

1. This poem was awarded the Debra Vazquez Excellence in Poetry Award from the Florida Community College Press Association, 2006.

Chapter Sixteen

Portfolios, Presentations, Aural Modeling, and Syllabi

Chapter by chapter, this book offers a foundation to mastering elements of craft required for writing artful poetry in contrast to verse or words on a page that are only one's uncontrolled emotions. This book has stressed art and artfulness; it offers fixed and free forms and defines most terms poets need to know. It has offered individual chapters on each primary element of craft.

This final chapter offers some useful information on how group facilitators might organize a series of classes or workshops in poetry, how each poet might compose and present his or her work, and how education professionals who need to create syllabi for their courses might use our chapters for a successful course on poetry.

We want to encourage people to use this book as they see fit. The chapters offer a variety of options for in and out of class work and study. The explications needn't be read in class but can be assigned for home reading. They can be used as models of poetic explication and as springboards for discussion. Pick and choose from the lessons. Some teachers have told us they prefer to lead the discussion of a poem in their own fashion. We understand that. We are all about artistic freedom.

PORTFOLIOS

During the last decade, the use of portfolios in the fine arts as well as in the humanities has gained interest. In a poetry workshop or poetry course, portfolios may be the best way to truly display one's breadth and depth of work. A portfolio is an artistic compilation of work; this compilation may be in an actual hardcover or softcover "container," such as an album or a chapbook-size manuscript, or a portfolio may be entirely electronic, one file that houses all separate documents.

Using both electronic and hard copy portfolios is certainly another option and a fine way to display and preserve one's poetry during a particular period of time.

The idea of using portfolios as an alternative assessment tool has garnered great respect in higher education as well as K–12 education recently. For teachers, we highly recommend using the display portfolio as the primary assessment tool rather than grading each individual poem assignment.

Grading individual poems makes writing them seem an academic rather than artistic exercise and indeed may stifle some poets from expression. In contrast, the portfolio of work can be assessed for a single grade at the end of a quarter or semester (or any workshop length) as a gestalt, a holistic oeuvre, as we argue art should be assessed.

We recommend offering several examples of completed and successful portfolios of different types at the beginning of each term (the first night). This says to students, here is how your writing will be evaluated and displayed.

Some of the portfolios that have been produced in our courses over the years include formally published chapbooks of sixteen to thirty-two pages; photographic-type albums with entries of poems instead of photos or juxtaposed with photos; sixteen to thirty-two pages of poems typed and printed with a formal title page and thematic title; an artistic collage of visual and poetic art on poster board or formal artist canvas(es); and PowerPoints (as well as printed copies of the PPs) incorporating electronic delivery of display.

If any teacher or facilitator wants to score portfolios in an academic fashion, here is some advice. We emphasize the word *display* in portfolios so that students understand their work is valued and respected no matter what level of artistry it reaches. The method for scoring portfolios should be discussed with students and clear to them as shown in a rubric or informally as notes on the board. For example, teachers might put a simple assessment scoring rubric on the board:

Sample Portfolio Rubric

Completion and display of 16–32 poems	33%
Artistic compilation of poems	33%
Presentation to class of portfolios	33%
	= 100%

Some educators may wish to assess quality of work by traditional grading methods; however, we argue against that method of assessment. Writers should be encouraged to create, to strive, to fail, and to master. If every poem earns a grade from A to F as in traditional grading methods, poets may be discouraged to "dare," to "leap," to attempt various forms and techniques, to even pour their work "out there" for group feedback and response.

For these reasons, we recommend poetry courses be graded as above. That score of the final display portfolio (plus a ten-minute presentation to the class) should equal individual participation in week-to-week class work of writing, critiquing, and sharing.

In other words, on the syllabus, poetry teachers might say a student's final grade will be determined as follows:

• 50 percent participation, including writing, submitting, sharing, and feedback on others' work
• 50 percent display portfolio (including all elements shown in the sample above)

It is obvious to us through our work with student writers of all ages at the college level that this kind of scoring and assessment is welcomed by students; indeed, we suggest that such an alternative assessment inspires creativity and improves participation and progress.

Teachers may choose to add individual notes on each student's progress before the portfolios are returned. We recommend teachers keep copies of various types of display portfolios through the first month of classes for subsequent semesters with permission from student writers. Thus, teachers can share as examples of portfolios those completed in a previous class. Most students are honored to share their portfolios in this fashion.

Portfolios for poets: We recommend all poets keep their work in organized portfolios with feedback and copies of revisions. Entries should be dated. Students may one day want to organize eighteen to thirty-two poems into a thematic chapbook to offer for publication. The portfolio will help them do this. Also, student writers can see their own growth as writers as they look back over earlier work; they can weed out and eliminate work that later seems below standard. Of course, we recommend an electronic portfolio too; in fact, best to keep two or three stored in various places.

LITERARY MAGAZINES

Teachers who wish to or who already serve as faculty advisors for their institution's student literary magazine can find another use for portfolios: selection of work to be included in the next issue. While many advisors do not have the final word in selection of poetry for inclusion, as that task is up to student editors and staff, advisors can select one or any number of poems from each student's portfolio to submit to the literary magazine student staff.

Many poets are hesitant to submit their work, so this strategy is an effective one. Also, it allows for the strongest work to at least be viewed by the staff of the magazine as selected by the teacher. Faculty advisors wear many hats—guides, mentors, editors, masters of writing, among others—and one of the most important is to nudge their student staff toward artistry of the highest level. Portfolios can be useful in this fashion too.

AURAL MODELING

The best scientifically based research on language and learning proves that aural modeling is one of the most effective teaching strategies. We recommend that the teacher read the model poem aloud to the class, using appropriate inflection, intonation, and prosody. Students learn from hearing a good reading; they begin to recognize poetic rhythms and hear meter.

They note alliteration and assonance and other sound devices. They see how the end of the line can be enjambed and how punctuation works.

As the class progresses and teachers assess and come to know the student poets, student readers can be chosen to read aloud. In our experience, students often like to read aloud after they have learned how to do it.

Some good readers are more dramatic than others. We have heard poets from Ted Kooser to Allen Ginsberg read aloud, and they are different in their use of voice and inflection, but all of them gave us the musicality of language and taught us more about what good poems are.

SYLLABI AND OTHER TYPES OF WORKSHOP ORGANIZATION

This book was purposefully organized into sixteen useful chapters that would work well for the traditional sixteen- or seventeen-week academic semester. Below is one way to organize any poetry course or workshop using this text.

SAMPLE SYLLABUS

Week 1:   Ch. 1. Some Initial Thoughts on Poets and Poetry
Introductory assignment in class or out: Ch. 1. Model Exercises 1

Week 2:   Ch. 2. Beyond the Ordinary: Witnessing the World as a Poet
Writing Assignment 1: Ch. 2. The Model Exercise

Week 3:   Ch. 3. Imagery: Getting to the Heart of It
Writing Assignment 2: Ch. 3. The Model Exercise

Week 4:   Ch. 4. Metaphors and Symbol: Finding and Using Creative Analogies
Writing Assignment 3: Ch. 4. The Model Exercise

Week 5:   Ch. 5. Line Endings, Turns, and Epiphanies: More Essential Elements of Craft
Writing Assignment 4: Ch. 5. The Model Exercise

Week 6:   Ch. 6. The Speaker and Reader: A Dialogue
Writing Assignment 5: Ch. 6. The Model Exercise

Week 7:   Ch. 7. Narrative Poetry: Poems That Tell Stories
Writing Assignment 6: Ch. 7. The Model Exercise

Week 8:   Ch. 8. Communicating Emotional Truths and Avoiding Melodrama
Writing Assignment 7: Ch. 8. The Model Exercise

Week 9:   Ch. 9. Writing in Other Voices
Writing Assignment 8: Ch. 9. The Model Exercise

Week 10:   Ch. 10. Sound Devices
Writing Assignment 9: Ch. 10. The Model Exercise

Week 11:   Ch. 11. Punctuation: A Surprisingly Creative Tool
Writing Assignment 10: Ch. 11. The Model Exercise

Week 12:   Ch. 12. Effective Titles: Hints at Theme
Writing Assignment 11: Ch. 12. The Model Exercise

Week 13:   Ch. 13. Nature as Muse
Writing Assignment 12: Ch. 13. The Model Exercise

Week 14:   Ch. 14. The Prose Poem: A Revelatory Form
Writing Assignment 13: Ch. 14. The Model Exercise

Week 15:   Ch. 15. Writing in Various Forms
Writing Assignment 14: Ch. 15. The Model Exercises (2 fixed forms of student or instructor choice)

Week 16:   Celebration & Presentation:

Display Portfolio Sharing

Students will present their portfolio, explaining how it is organized and collected, and read three poems to the class. (Formal podium presentations recommended.) Students might wish to invite friends or relatives. Teachers might enjoy providing an informal tea with refreshments and snacks for all.

No final exam. The alternative assessment display portfolio serves as the evaluative exam.

Alternate Week 16: Sharing/workshopping of fixed-form poem exercise. Discussion and preparation for final night celebration (see above).

Alternate Week 17: Celebration and Presentation:

Display Portfolio Sharing—Students will present their portfolio, explaining how it is organized and collected, and read three poems to the class. (Formal podium presentations recommended.) Students might wish to invite friends or relatives. Teachers might enjoy providing an informal tea with refreshments and snacks for all.

No final exam. The alternative assessment display portfolio serves as the evaluative exam.

ALTERNATE SYLLABI

This book can be used for two semesters by taking two weeks on each chapter's reading, exercises, and workshopping experience. Chapters 1 through 8 plus final portfolio and sharing for semester A and chapters 9 through 15 for semester B with final portfolio and sharing.

Also, as we have done at both national conferences and local workshops, any chapter in this book may be used as an individual workshop lasting two to six hours.

Brief Literary
Biographies of the Poets

Robert Browning (1812–1889) Originally an unsuccessful playwright, Browning turned his craft to poetry, writing a number of remarkable dramatic monologues, including "My Last Duchess." Born in England, he was married to fellow poet Elizabeth Barrett Browning.

Emily Dickinson (1830–1886) Born into an influential, wealthy New England family, Dickinson spent the majority of her life in Amherst, Massachusetts, and much of it in an elegant manor house just past the village green. She never married, and some critics proclaim her a recluse, but Dickinson had an unusual personality that has yet to be quite adequately defined by biographies. Dickinson's verse, completely ignored in her lifetime, gained fame and value fifty or more years after her death, particularly with the publication of the Johnson edition of her poems with reinstated dashes and use of capital letters from her original writings. She was a free spirit and individualist whose sharp eye, sensibility, and intelligence created poetry quite unparalleled.

Robert Frost (1874–1963) Though born in San Francisco, Frost became identified with Yankees and New England, once saying he intended to return there from Europe and "grow Yankee-er and Yankee-er." He was briefly an expatriate in England from 1912 to 1915. Educated at Dartmouth and a student though not a graduate of Harvard, Frost is—one might argue—the most influential and well-known poet of the modern era (or perhaps any era in American literature). His poetry is sophisticated philosophical query; its style, manner, and voice are completely unique. Though a rebellious spirit in some ways, he claimed he preferred to write in fixed forms because to write without them would be "like playing tennis with the net down." His humor, wit, and dark wisdom are evident in his work.

Lola Haskins is a Florida-based poet whose work, written and spoken, has been heralded by critics and readers alike. She was a professor at the University of Florida in the Computers and Informational Technology Department. Haskins is the author of eight books of poetry, one of which won the Iowa Poetry Prize (*Hunger*, 1993). She is the recipient of two fellowships from the NEA and four individual artist fellowships from the State of Florida.

Robert Hayden (1913–1980) Born in Detroit, Michigan, Hayden was a professor of English. His work focuses on black civil rights but also offers singular insights into blue-collar, working-class family life.

Jane Kenyon (1947–1995) Born in Michigan, Kenyon was married to poet Donald Hall from 1972 until her death of leukemia in New Hampshire. Hall and Kenyon lived at Hall's family farm, where she was deeply influenced by nature, animals, and rural life. She published four collections of her own poems; she translated twenty poems by Russian poet Anna Akhmatova.

Ted Kooser (1939) An American poet born in Iowa, Kooser was educated at Iowa State University and the University of Nebraska. Kooser writes of daily life with extraordinary detail and analysis. His use of metaphor is unparalleled in American poetry. He was named Poet Laureate of the United States from 2004 to 2006 and maintains a weekly national column in poetry.

W. S. Merwin (1927) William Stanley Merwin, poet, playwright, and novelist, has won the Pulitzer Prize in Poetry twice, in 1971 and 2009, among other honors. Merwin lives in Hawaii, where he is actively involved in ecology awareness and rainforest protection. His poetry exhibits a Zen-like quality that illustrates his interest in nature, creatures, and the mysteries of creation. His poems, particularly for the past several decades, reject traditional forms, meters, and rhymes, containing instead their own unique prosody.

Mary Oliver (1935) Oliver was born in Cleveland and educated at Vassar College and Ohio State University. Her work has received a number of high honors, including the National Book Award, the Shelley Memorial Award, and the Pulitzer Prize in Poetry. She lives in Provincetown and teaches at Bennington College.

William Shakespeare (1564–1616) Shakespeare, arguably the greatest of all English-speaking poets and writers, is credited with 154 sonnets in addition to numerous plays. His biography is shrouded in mystery, and some scholars have advanced arguments that he was actually of royal birth rather than the Catholic son of a merchant in Stratford on Avon. Unquestionably, however, he influenced and forwarded the sonnet form and rhythmic, lyrical poetry.

William Stafford (1914–1993) Kansas-born Stafford published sixty-three books, including *The Rescued Year* (1966), *Stories That Could Be True: New and Collected Poems* (1977), and *An Oregon Message* (1987). His book *Traveling through the Dark* won the National Book Award in 1963. Stafford moved to Oregon in 1948. He taught at Lewis and Clark College until his retirement in 1980.

Dylan Thomas (1914–1953) Born in Wales, Thomas earned fame as a poet and as a dramatic reader of his own poems, which are musical and lyrical in nature and sound. Thomas spent some time in New York City's Greenwich Village and published two major books of poetry in his lifetime before dying of alcohol-related disease. His poem "Do Not Go Gentle into That Good Night" was set to music by John Cale in the Falklands Suite. *The Poems of Dylan Thomas* was posthumously published in 1971.

Jean Valentine (1934) Born in Chicago, Valentine is the recipient of numerous distinguished awards for writers, including but not limited to a Guggenheim Fellowship and the Teasdale Memorial Prize. She has taught at Sarah Lawrence College, New York University, and Columbia University.

Richard Wilbur (1921) Born in New York City, Wilbur served in World War II in the U.S. Army and later attended Harvard University. A translator of major French writers as well as a poet, Wilbur has earned the Wallace Stevens Award, the Frost Medal, and the Gold Medal Award from the American Academy of Arts and Letters. He was awarded the Pulitzer Prize in Poetry and the National Book Award, among other distinctions.

James Wright (1927–1980) An Ohio native, Wright earned a Ph.D. at the University of Washington, where he was a student of Theodore Roethke. In 1972, he won the Pulitzer Prize for Poetry for his *Collected Poems* (1971). Dr. Wright taught at Hunter College in New York City.

Sir Thomas Wyatt (1503–1542) An English nobleman who entered the court of Henry VIII in 1516, where he ultimately became infatuated with Anne Boleyn. Wyatt was knighted in 1535 but imprisoned at least once for various charges against the crown. He has been credited with introducing the sonnet form to English poetry.

Gary Young (1951) founded Greenhouse Review Press and teaches at the University of California at Santa Cruz. He is a recipient of the National Endowment for the Humanities and is a poet, printer, and artist.

Yvonne Zipter (1954) was born in Milwaukee. Her poetry books include *Diamonds Are a Dyke's Best Friend*, which explores softball in the lesbian community, and *The Patience of Metal*, which was a Chicago Book Clinic Honor Book. Zipter contributes to *The Skinny: Greyhounds Only Newsletter*, of which she is very proud.